MW01492595

Gambling on a Dream

Gambling on a Dream

THE CLASSIC LAS VEGAS STRIP
1930-1955

Lynn M. Zook

AMERICA
THROUGH TIME®
ADDING COLOR TO AMERICAN HISTORY

America Through Time is an imprint of Fonthill Media LLC
www.through-time.com
office@through-time.com

Published by Arcadia Publishing by arrangement with Fonthill Media LLC
For all general information, please contact Arcadia Publishing:
Telephone: 843-853-2070
Fax: 843-853-0044
E-mail: sales@arcadiapublishing.com
For customer service and orders:
Toll-Free 1-888-313-2665

www.arcadiapublishing.com

First published 2018

Copyright © Lynn M. Zook 2018

ISBN 978-1-63499-067-7

All rights reserved. No part of this publication may be reproduced, stored in a retrieval system or transmitted in any form or by any means, electronic, mechanical, photocopying, recording or otherwise, without prior permission in writing from Fonthill Media LLC

Typeset in Minion Pro 10pt on 13pt
Printed in the United States of America

The products featured in this book are from the author's
As We Knew It: Classic Las Vegas Collection unless otherwise noted.
Cover Design and Hotel Location Maps by Joanna Arlukiewicz.

DEDICATION

To my folks, Dan and Laura Zook, for having the foresight to raise a family in Las Vegas and teaching us to always follow our dreams.

And to the love of my life, Jon Stromp, for all his love and support that helped make this book possible.

CONTENTS

ACKNOWLEDGMENTS

This book would not have been possible without the support of a numerous people.

The men and women who participated in the Classic Las Vegas History Project and shared their stories about living and working in Las Vegas in the post-war era were invaluable. They shared not only their stories but often rare photos and other memorabilia. I am forever grateful for their participation in the project and the friendships that came out of that project.

My good friend, author Alan Hess, whose seminal book, *Viva Las Vegas: After-Hours Architecture*, remains one of the best books about the architecture of that era, for the inspiration to tell this story.

A much deserved thank you to my scarecrow, Dennis McBride, whose preservation work served as the inspiration for my Classic Las Vegas journey, and the staff of the Nevada State Museum, Las Vegas. I truly appreciate all the help and thank you for allowing me to use images from the J. Florian Mitchell and Cliff Segerblom Collections as well as other images from the Nevada State Museum, Las Vegas Photographic Collections.

A special thank you to Su Kim Chung and UNLV Special Collections for all their help and support.

A special thank you to writer Pete Hamill, whose writings on the New York City he knew served as a touchstone, for generously giving his permission to be quoted.

George Stamos for sharing with me his collection of the stories he wrote for the *Las Vegas Sun Sunday Magazine* that provided invaluable information about the original hotels.

To Bo Boisvert, Carey Burke, Joel Rosales, and Allen Sandquist, all who work to help preserve the Las Vegas of our collective memory, for sharing and allowing me to use images from their personal collections.

To Shannon Clute for the mentoring, Christina Putnam-Cox for her much appreciated effort in editing, Moira Finnie Neylon and Alexa Foreman for their continued support, and Dr. Michael Green for taking on the Herculean task of final proofing. I would be remiss if I did not thank my good friend and neon preservationist, Eric Lynxwiler.

I also want to thank my parents, Dan and Laura Zook, who in making the move to Las Vegas in the early 1960s, made it possible for me to grow up there in that wonderful era.

And most importantly, to my husband, Jon Stromp, for his unwavering support and love throughout this process. His dogged insistence made this project possible.

Thank you to every one who helped make this book possible and to those who read it and enjoyed the trip back in time! Image courtesy of the J. Florian Mitchell Collection, Nevada State Museum, Las Vegas.

FOREWORD
BY ALAN HEISS

The strange and strained relationship between Las Vegas and the architectural establishment has distorted perceptions of the city for decades.

On the one hand, the architects and sign designers and their clients who established the template for the Las Vegas Strip lead the nation in inventing new building types to respond to the automobile, and to the new leisure and recreation economy; they responded instantly to the latest demographic trends in the Sunbelt's growing suburban metropolises, pioneered the practical theory of signs and semeiotics, and took those ideas about as far as they could be taken.

Some of the hotels were among the largest ever built; some used creative new technical achievements (like engineer T. Y. Lin's prestressed concrete slabs at the Stardust's room wings); some advanced theater design to stage astonishing spectacles; almost all blended signage and structure into one seamless architecture that reimagined urban design for the midcentury's suburban metropolises.

Yet none of these innovations were reported in the major professional architecture journals. They found almost no mention in any of the histories written in those times.

By all rights Wayne McAllister, George Vernon Russell, Kermit Wayne, and the others should have been stars of the design professions for perfecting a remarkable and practical new form in the 1950s—the automobile-oriented motel-entertainment center. Even well-known architects who usually attracted the attention of the journals (Pereira & Luckman, Welton Becket, Douglas Honnold) could not (or would not) convince the editors of *Architectural Record* or *Architectural Forum* to publish their Las Vegas work. McAllister, the most innovative trailblazer of them all for his designs for the 1941 El Rancho Vegas (the first Strip hotel, built by Thomas Hull), the 1952 Sands, and the 1956 Fremont Hotel, labored entirely in obscurity until the 1990s.

It did not have to be so. We were warned. Outside of the professional journals, smart observers saw something significant in the Strip. As early as 1956 geographer

J. B. Jackson pointed our attention toward neon signs and the urbanism of popular taste. Tom Wolfe visited Las Vegas in 1965 and told us that something spectacular in terms of art was going on there. Reyner Banham in 1970 wrote of the electric city, the precursor of the electronic urbanism of today. Robert Venturi, Denise Scott Brown, and Steven Izenour laid it all out for us in 1972 in *Learning From Las Vegas;* instead of opening our eyes to a practical and visceral urbanism, though, its message was usually sidetracked into theoretical discussions. My own contribution, *Viva Las Vegas: After-Hours Architecture* (1993), was meager compared to those illustrious observers, but it captured the factual history, the images of the actual buildings, and the stories of their designers at long last.

Why was Las Vegas blacked out of the architectural press and professional discussion? The question deserves a dissertation. One possible cause was the pointed distaste held by the east coast's gatekeeper editors for anything to do with gambling and popular life. Or it could be that the many unsavory characters who financed and ran the hotels in Las Vegas' initial creative phase put many people off—even while mainstream figures like Conrad Hilton, Del Webb, and Howard Hughes were involved with its development.

I think the main reason was this: the professional journals, academies, and critics of the time may have said they were in favor of Modern ideas, but they had qualms about their implications if allowed to blossom fully. To keep a tight hold on the reins, the critics simply ignored Las Vegas.

This blackout has had a long-term impact on American architecture. It robbed the architecture profession of some of the most original thinking on the major urban issue of the day: how to design suburbia. Though Las Vegas is no ordinary suburb, its extraordinary environment (enormous budgets, large scale, wide open spaces, free-thinking clients, auto orientation) allowed those ideas to be tested and refined.

Still, the lack of critical attention may have been an advantage. Like other Sunbelt cities (only more so), Las Vegas was at ease with the fast pace of change, and with practicality—and always with imagination. There was a complete and utter absence of any architectural establishment, critics, or academics to slow them down with concerns for precedents or theoretical niceties. Strip architects, sign designers, and builders were able to see and address problems before them clearly and directly. As it turned out—and this may be the element of pure luck that blessed Las Vegas—many of these architects and designers were brilliantly creative. Presented with the challenge of inventing a new architectural type, and given sizable budgets (there were almost always sizable budgets), and the freedom to design as they saw fit, they used the opportunity to exercise their genius.

Once they satisfied the functional parameters of a hotel (the number of rooms, the size and convenience of the parking lot) these designers could focus their

Sketch of the original Sands sign and hotel. Image courtesy of UNLV's Special Collections.

attention on everything else: the intimacy of the restaurants, the timelessness of the casinos, the vividness of the roadside sign, the relaxation of the swimming pool landscape. Weaving all of these competing elements together properly amounted to designing something with the complexity of a small city. So successful were their solutions in the 1950s, though, that when Strip hotels had grown enormous in the 1970s, their basic strategies still worked.

These creative solutions can be seen up and down the Strip throughout its history: Wayne McAllister's initial inspiration to take the simple roadside motel (rooms, lobby, parking, sign, pool) and grow it into the luxurious El Rancho Vegas resort in the middle of nowhere; Kermit Wayne's transformation of an ordinary roadside billboard into an evocative animated neon sign depicting the known universe and all its stars and planets at the Stardust; Martin Stern, Jr.'s influential tri-winged International Hotel.

These architects and designers determined the way to integrate scale, imagery, cars, convenience, and even a human scale on the armature of the commercial strip. They established a tradition (*The Las Vegas School*, if you will) based on Las Vegas' strengths (signs, symbols, spaces, sidewalks, and attractions), and handed it down through the decades. You can see that tradition's impact continuing into the 1990s where Jon Jerde's Bellagio and Joel Bergman's Caesars Palace (elaborating on Jay Sarno's original concept) and Paris intersect at one of the greatest postindustrial urban spaces, at the corner of the Strip and Flamingo. The chaotic design of CityCenter, opened in 2009, is a harsh reminder that cities suffer when they ignore their past. CityCenter imported famous architects and the sleek scaleless mirrored glass that is fashionable globally today, but they ignored the rich popular imagery that worked so well for the Aladdin, the Sands, the Dunes, and the Stardust. They built cliffs along the sidewalks where there was once open space, and undermined the pleasures of pedestrianism.

The lessons of Las Vegas' early visionaries, unchained by conventions, has been lost to much of the current generation.

In the beginning, the builders and designers of the Las Vegas Strip had the freedom to solve problems pragmatically, and the creativity to turn their solutions into art. They understood the car, and the proper scale of buildings seen from the car, the artistic potential of the sign, and its role in organizing urban space across broad prospects.

It was a similar pragmatism and art, freed from tradition, that inspired earlier Modern architects to invent the skyscraper. Both the Strip and skyscrapers required the application of new technologies, a new sense of urbanism, and the creativity to see their visionary possibilities. Both turned out to be tremendously influential in the development of architecture and cities, yet only the skyscraper is honored in the history books.

Will the Strip ever be granted the same prestige?

Looking north from the Sands Hotel, Highway 91 was the precursor of the fabulous Las Vegas Strip. Image courtesy of the J. Florian Mitchell collection, Nevada State Museum, LasVegas.

INTRODUCTION

Nostalgia is not a fake emotion. It is an ache for something that did exist. It involves an almost fatalistic acceptance of the permanent presence of loss. Nothing will ever stay the same. Tuesday turns into Wednesday and something valuable is behind you forever. An "is" has become a "was."

Pete Hamill, *Downtown: My Manhattan*

LAS VEGAS

I had the good fortune to grow up in that mythical place during its heyday as the "Entertainment Capital of the World" all the while never fully appreciating the role it plays in our collective memory.

It wasn't until many years later when it began to be destroyed that I finally understood how important it had been and how it's slow destruction could break our hearts.

Today, with its mega-resorts, it's hard to imagine now how different the famous Las Vegas Strip looked back then. Looking at pictures now, it seems almost quaint. But, those pictures only begin to hint at the allure and pull that Las Vegas and this five-mile strip of highway had on the American imagination in the years following World War II.

Beginning in the 1930s and through the 1970s, the Strip hotels were designed for the automobile driver. They had huge neon signs that beckoned you to pull off the highway, come out of the heat, and stay for a while. The long driveways led to shaded *porte cocheres* where bellmen raced to unload your car and take your bags. Swanky air-conditioned lobbies could be seen through the ceiling to floor glass windows.

Back then, people didn't typically walk the Strip the way they do today. The empty land between the properties was often larger than it looked and made walking, especially in the summer heat, all but impossible. The original dreamers that had staked their claim to this five-mile strip of desert, along with world-class entertainers, and the talented photographers of the Las Vegas News Bureau, helped make Las Vegas a major tourist destination.

Dotting the landscape amidst all that open space were dozens of small motels, often family-owned and operated. Motels such as the Lone Palm, the Desert Rose, the Mirage (which later became the Glass Pool), the Kit Carson, the Desert Villa, and many others, are now all lost to history. There were gas stations like Texaco, Phillips 66, Gulf, and Standard promising the road-weary traveler that they would not run out of gas before getting to their destination. On the trip home, they offered aspirin to cure the inevitable hang-over. Restaurants like the Villa Roma and Luigi's were also part of the mix along with the occasional liquor stores, early sports books, and bars.

But most of all, there was neon everywhere.

From the giant hotel marquees that announced to the world who was gracing their showroom stages to the smaller motels, neon was king on the Strip. Every hotel had a large marquee sign and some, like the Sahara, retained their smaller, original roadside signage as well. The Texaco station at the Hotel Last Frontier had a fire truck in moving neon. The Silver Slipper had its large rotating Slipper and a large marquee sign with the outline of a working slot machine.

The motel and restaurant signs all competed with moving neon signs in bright, primary colors that made traveling down the Strip all the way to downtown's Fremont Street an eye-popping kaleidoscope of color, lights, movement and neon.

Those days are gone now and while we can catch glimpses of them in classic movies and televisions shows, it is an era that mainly exists in our collective memory.

Almost all the original hotels have been destroyed and the few that remain are endangered. The large neon signs, for the most part, have been destroyed or, if lucky, have found a home in the city's Neon Museum's bone yard awaiting restoration. Large LCD screens have replaced the neon and wonderment as the Las Vegas Strip has evolved from the swanky home of the Rat Pack to what Americans want from their favorite vacation resorts in the twenty-first century.

But it wasn't always that way.

The Las Vegas Strip of today owes a large debt to the men who dreamed large and who saw, almost from the beginning, the potential for this five-mile stretch of desert to become America's playground.

Without them, none of what follows would have been possible.

The Welcome to Las Vegas sign by neon designer, Betty Willis. Image courtesy of the As We Knew It: Classic Las Vegas Collection.

1

THE EARLY YEARS

It wasn't gambling and Lady Luck that first lured people to Las Vegas; it was the water. Water had long sustained the Paiutes who called the region home; it had sustained the early explorers along the old Spanish Trail and the Mormon Trail.

Homesteaders like Archibald and Helen Stewart soon followed and they created a way station for travelers at their ranch. It was water that brought Montana Senator William A. Clark to Las Vegas. His railroad line, the San Pedro, Los Angeles and Salt Lake, needed a water stop between the City of Angels and Salt Lake City, almost 700 miles apart. Las Vegas, with its abundant water that flowed from the Big Springs just west of the little town that was home to about thirty people, got his attention.

He persuaded widow Helen Stewart to sell her ranch and for $55,000 he acquired 1,800 acres with only a $5,000 down payment. In addition, for no extra money, he obtained the Las Vegas Springs, the ranch's main water supply and home to the Big Springs. He had dreams of turning the small town into a model railroad town complete with staging area for his main railroad, a storage area, and small lots that would include housing for his workers.

The land auction on May 15, 1905 was a two-day affair with bidding brisk for both commercial and residential lots, and the town of Las Vegas was officially born. In 1909, the state legislators voted to create a new county that they named after the Montana senator who had brought the railroad to the sparsely populated Las Vegas valley. Within two years of the County's designation, over 1,500 people called Las Vegas home, with 450 of them working for Clark's railroad.

A national rail strike, coupled with economic hard times in 1922, almost crippled the rail line. Clark sold his holdings to the larger Union Pacific and scabs were sent in to break the strike line. When eighteen rail workers were arrested, trains were idled in Las Vegas. The effect on the economy of the town was severe. Following the strike, the Union Pacific moved the repair yards to Caliente and 300 Las Vegas railroad workers lost their jobs.

William Clark waves from his private rail car. Image courtesy of the Bracken Collection, UNLV's Special Collections.

May 15, 1905: Land Auction in Las Vegas. Image courtesy of the Nevada State Museum, Las Vegas.

Luckily, the men and women who called the dusty little railroad town home refused to give up on it. They continued to go about their daily lives, raising families and often struggling to keep their businesses afloat and food on the table.

In 1931, the state legislature passed a bill legalizing gambling throughout the state with the hope that this would lure gamblers to come and visit. When the bill passed, Nevada became the only state with legal gaming. While gambling went on in other states, it was considered illegal and local and federal law enforcement kept an eye out for back room and speakeasy gambling. Meanwhile in Nevada, Reno mainly reaped the benefits of a steady cash flow from losing gamblers. In Las Vegas, small gambling joints, like the Northern Club on Fremont Street, began to spring up.

With Prohibition in full swing, speakeasies and juke joints helped fill the entertainment void. And in Las Vegas, where the summer heat sometimes thrives in triple digits, a cold drink was more than tempting. Locals tended to turn a blind eye towards the lax support of the national liquor ban, and, in a way, that attitude set the stage for all that would come along that desolate two-lane blacktop that connected Las Vegas to California.

THE 1930s

Before Tommy Hull and the El Rancho Vegas and long before Bugsy Siegel drove up the highway and had that so-called fever dream, there was the Pair-O-Dice Club. Local residents Frank and Angelina Detra purchased the land in early 1930 and opened the Pair-O-Dice as a private nightclub.

The Pair-O-Dice Club. Image courtesy of the Nevada State Museum, Las Vegas.

The area around the Pair-O-Dice Club. Image courtesy of the Nevada State Museum, Las Vegas.

Highway 91, also known as the LA Highway, brought customers from Southern California. Prohibition was still in effect when the Club opened, and legalized gambling was still a year away, so it not only offered illegal games of chance but also had a speakeasy serving illegal alcohol. The Detras had a copper distillery hidden under the quail pen in the back of the property. Since Frank Detra was a friend and associate of Chicago crime boss Al Capone, federal agents scrutinized the Detras and their Club, but, unlike the nearby Red Rooster, they did not raid the Pair-O-Dice.

When Nevada legalized gambling in 1931, the Detras' illegal gambling sideline suddenly became a legal business. The owners had hoped to obtain the first gaming license issued to a county business, but that honor went to their neighbor and rival, the Red Rooster, which was located a mile south on the highway and was the first club motorists saw as they approached Las Vegas.

The Pair-O-Dice was issued its gaming license on May 5, 1931, and the Detras installed a roulette wheel, a craps table, and a blackjack table. The venue smoothly transitioned from a private club to a public one within the month and it continued to serve alcohol, albeit quietly. When Prohibition was repealed in 1933, the Club obtained a license to serve beer, and it became more popular with locals and tourists than the nearby Red Rooster. The popularity of the Pair-O-Dice was due largely to the gourmet Italian restaurant that was part of the Club. The food was served on fine china with silver utensils and real linen tablecloths with lace napkins designed by Angelina Detra. The Club also featured entertainment, so it became popular with the dinner and dancing crowd.

The facade was Spanish style with rounded archways, a tile roof, and an octagonal-shaped entryway. It also featured an intricate swamp cooling system, which proved very popular with their customers in the summer months of stifling heat. In 1938, the Detras sold the property to Guy McAfee, a former vice squad captain from Los Angeles who left Southern California under a cloud of suspicion when it was discovered he owned shares in various gambling and prostitution rings there.

McAfee is credited with coining the name "the Strip." He had frequented the clubs along the famed Sunset Strip in Los Angeles and knew it was only a matter of time before the landscape here in Las Vegas would be dotted with the clubs and entertainment.

McAfee, with an eye towards the Southern California crowd and the nightclubs they liked to frequent, changed the name to the 91 Club. He made the interior more lavish, hired a larger orchestra and replaced the gourmet Italian food with affordable steak dinners. He also emphasized the gaming more. McAfee opened the new club in 1939, delaying the opening to coincide with the Clark Gable-Ria Langham divorce. Langham had come to Las Vegas to establish her six-week residency in order to get the divorce.

Tommy Hull began construction on the El Rancho Vegas, the first modern hotel and casino on "the Strip," one mile north of the 91 Club in 1940. By 1941,

Guy McAfee, on the left, with friends. Image courtesy of the Nevada State Museum, Las Vegas.

Alice Morris, on the right, and friend in front of the Red Rooster, 1934. Image courtesy of the Nevada State Museum, Las Vegas.

R. E. Griffith was scouting locations for his new hotel, the Hotel Last Frontier, and bought the 91 Club. McAfee took that money, went downtown and invested in the Golden Nugget on Fremont Street, among others.

Despite Prohibition, Las Vegas in the early 1930s was notorious for thumbing its nose at the law and allowing consumption of alcohol in local clubs. Though Fremont Street was very popular with the locals, Highway 91 offered tourists, who were tired after that long drive from Southern California, a chance to quench their thirsts.

Alice Wilson Morris opened the Red Rooster Club in 1931. It had a Spanish-style mission façade that offered a stage, dance floor and dining area. But, in the early 1930s, it was better known for its speakeasy.

In February 1931, the U.S. Justice Department ordered the Red Rooster Club's owner to comply with an order to stop serving alcohol; if the order wasn't heeded, federal agents would shut the Club down. The famed Arizona Club on Fremont Street had recently been shut down for the same non-compliance. Morris complied with the order, at least in the beginning.

In March, the Red Rooster received the first County gaming license and installed a blackjack table and three slot machines. But the gaming didn't last long because reports of illegal alcohol being served at the Club were rampant.

In July, the Red Rooster was raided by federal agents and charged with illegally selling alcohol. In the aftermath, Morris lost her gaming license.

Two years later, Morris had a new plan. She received a license from the County to run the Red Rooster as a dance hall. When Prohibition was repealed, the County gave the Club a liquor license but only to serve beer.

On July 8, a cook arriving to work discovered a fire in the rear of the building. The building burned to the ground, but, luckily for Morris, it was insured. The rebuilt Red Rooster opened on that New Year's Eve and remained popular throughout the rest of the 1930s and World War II.

Former stage and film star Grace Hayes bought the club in 1947 and renamed it the Grace Hayes Lodge. Benjamin Siegel was reportedly a frequent customer in the 1940s. Hayes sold the property in 1950 but then bought it back a year later. An auto court/small motel named the Sans Souci was added to the property.

Hayes finally sold the property for good in 1953. The northern end of the L.A. highway was undergoing a construction boom and she quickly found a buyer.

The Las Vegas Strip was growing.

Bungalows at the Grace Hayes Lodge. Image courtesy of the J. Florian Mitchell Collection, Nevada State Museum, Las Vegas.

2

THE EL RANCHO VEGAS
1941-1960

STOP AT THE SIGN OF THE WINDMILL

Like so much of Las Vegas history, this story begins with a tall tale:

For decades, the story has been that hotelier Tommy Hull's car broke down on the old LA Highway (Highway 91) near San Francisco Avenue (now Sahara Avenue). It was a hot day with the sun beating down. While waiting for a tow truck, Hull counted the cars that drove by and envisioned a swimming pool that fronted on the highway that would invite weary, sweaty travelers to stop at his hotel and casino.

It's a good story but it's a myth.

Tommy Hull was friends with Las Vegas civic booster extraordinaire, "Big Jim" Cashman. Hull had a chain of successful El Rancho hotels in California, and he operated the Roosevelt Hotel in Hollywood. Cashman worked hard to convince Hull that he should build one of his El Rancho Hotels in Las Vegas. One night over drinks at the Hotel Apache on Fremont Street, Hull finally agreed with Cashman. It was 1939 and Las Vegas was still a small town. A few gambling halls and hotels dotted Fremont Street downtown, but nothing on the scale of one of Hull's El Rancho hotels.

Hull priced property in Las Vegas and then turned his eye to the County property on the other side of San Francisco Avenue. Mrs. Jessie Hunt owned the property, and she thought it was worthless. She had thirty-three acres that she was all but ready to give away. Wanting to get the most for his investment, Hull bought the property—and an additional thirty-three acres—at a cost of $150 per acre on the southwest corner of San Francisco Avenue (today Sahara Avenue) and Highway 91 (today Las Vegas Blvd. South).

From the beginning, Hull envisioned a ranch-style property with a main casino, dining room, a showroom, and a lounge. In addition, he envisioned hotel rooms where people could drive up and park their cars near their rooms or bungalows and relax at the nearby enticing swimming pool amid the sprawling landscaped

The El Rancho Vegas, the first hotel on the Las Vegas Strip. Image courtesy of UNLV's Special Collections.

lawns. He knew that after spending hours of driving from Southern California, in those days before air-conditioning in cars, people would be tired of seeing the desert, and the El Rancho would entice travelers like the proverbial oasis.

Hull hired famed Los Angeles architect Wayne McAllister of the firm McAllister and McAllister. The first rendering closely matched the finished complex. The neon-lit windmill atop the main building would become its trademark. In those early days, when the desert seemed to go on forever, the neon signage could be seen for miles. The buildings were all painted white, and the grounds landscaped with green grass, flowers, and palm trees.

Construction of the hotel began in 1940. The architecture was predominantly frontier style with some popular Spanish mission style flourishes thrown in for flavoring. A rustic frontier style was applied to the main building, to the shops, and to the numerous bungalows and cottages that encircled the main building. All the buildings were painted white to reflect the relentless summer sun. Brown shingle roofing was added to the main building while the bungalows featured red tile roofs. This, of course, became a major factor in the survival of the buildings twenty years later.

Inside, the Wagon Wheel Tavern offered old-fashioned chuck wagon dinners, and the decor was straight out of a Hollywood Western set with wagon wheels

The front of the El Rancho Vegas. Image courtesy of the Nevada State Museum, Las Vegas.

and hitching posts. There was the Stage Door Steak House, the Nugget Nell Cocktail Lounge, and the Round-Up Room dining room and showroom. The casino was small compared to the 300-seat showroom and only offered two blackjack tables, one roulette table, one craps table, and seventy slot machines. Again, the decor mirrored a Hollywood western with wagon-wheel chandeliers.

While the windmill dominated the exterior of the building, the Round-Up Room dominated the interior of the main building and, in some ways, overshadowed the casino area. There was a dance floor that doubled as the main stage. Small hurricane lamps with stitched leather shades and chairs adorned in similar leather effects completed the rustic frontier feeling.

A wishing well, with its own bucket, was against one wall and was a popular destination for young and old hoping to find "Mr. or Miss Right."

Chaise lounges and a brightly designed verandah, where swimmers could get a cool drink after swimming in the turquoise water, surrounded the famed pool. Colorful beams supported the verandah's canopy. The sun arbor, a trellis with white wooden beams, was filled with an explosion of bright-colored flowers. Riding stables located in the back of the property offered guests the opportunity to go horseback riding.

The El Rancho Vegas opened on April 3, 1941, and most of Las Vegas, it seems, showed up for the gala opening. Highway 91 was a rough, pot-holed, two-lane blacktop road in those days, so getting there was a bit of hike from downtown,

Guests were shuttled to their rooms. Image courtesy of the Nevada State Museum, Las Vegas.

not to mention a bumpy ride. Hull hired a troupe of showgirls and had them dressed in scanty western attire. Bandleader Garwood Van, who would later own one of the premiere music stores in town, Garwood Van's Musicland, and his Orchestra, were hired for four weeks.

"We had the first production show with Frank Fay and Ernie Rayburn, 'El Rancho Starlets.'" recalled Van in a 1979 interview with *Las Vegas Sun* reporter, George Stamos. "Hull said to me how beautiful Vegas was in the winter, but I said, 'who works in Vegas?' But after being signed for only four weeks I ended up staying for 13 months!" (*Las Vegas Sun Sunday Magazine*, April 1, 1979)

According to Van, the place was jam-packed from opening night on. "I was absolutely amazed at the number of people that came. Highway 91 was so busted up if you went over 40 miles per hour, you'd break an axle." (*Las Vegas Sun Sunday Magazine*, April 1, 1979)

Tommy Hull approached local business owner Maxwell Kelch with an offer. Kelch and his wife, Laura Belle, owned KENO radio and had been transmitting out of the burned hull of the old Meadows nightclub out on Boulder Highway. Hull offered Kelch some land behind the hotel for his radio station. Their daughter, Marilyn Gubler, recounted the story for the author in a 2005 interview:

The first station was where Boulder Highway, Fremont Street and Charleston all come together down there. And it had been an old nightclub, and they rented

An ad for Keno Radio which transmitted from the grounds of the El Rancho Vegas. Image courtesy of As We Knew It: Classic Las Vegas Collection.

that facility, and that's where they started the station. But then Tommy Hull was building the El Rancho and he called daddy and he said, "Max, how would you like to come and bring your station, if I move everything for you, the towers, the transmitters, I'll give you free studio space if you'd like to come and be in our hotel." And Daddy didn't have to think much about that, (he) immediately said yes and of course Tommy got the benefit of every twenty minutes on the station break.

When all the people were driving in from L.A. and listening to the only station, they could hear, "This is radio station K-E-N-O coming to you from the grounds of the fabulous El Rancho Vegas." So it was a nice win-win for Tommy Hull and for Daddy.

When World War II broke out, Hull arranged for servicemen at the over-crowded Gunnery School, today Nellis Air Force Base, to stay at the El Rancho. They built an additional sixty units to accommodate the military and the rooms were never empty.

In 1942, actress Carole Lombard, her mother, and her press agent (along with nineteen other passengers) were flying home from a cross-country War Bonds Drive. Lombard and her party were supposed to go by train, but Lombard was eager to get home to her husband, movie idol Clark Gable. They had a fight before she left for the tour and she hadn't said goodbye. She never made it back to Los Angeles. The plane crashed into Mt. Potosi shortly after taking off from the airport in North Las Vegas. Out in Searchlight at the Walking Box Ranch, western movie star Rex Bell and his foreman saw the smoke from the crash, loaded their horse trailers, and started toward the mountain, hoping they could be of help. Bell's wife, silent film star Clara Bow, and their son, Rex, Jr., watched the smoke from the balcony of their ranch house.

Clark Gable, upon receiving the news, rushed to Las Vegas in hopes that Lombard and the others would be found alive. He stayed at the El Rancho Vegas. Gable wanted to accompany the search and rescue team but was physically restrained from going. Reports are that he paced the floor of his bungalow awaiting word. When word came that Ms. Lombard and everyone on board had perished, Gable wired his frequent co-star, Spencer Tracy. Tracy came at once to help his friend. He, too, stayed at the El Rancho where the two were seen drinking into the night. Once the funeral arrangements were made, Gable and Tracy headed back to Los Angeles.

It was Hull's intention to make his resort self-contained. Anything the guests needed, his staff was there to be sure they were accommodated. It was a departure from the thinking of the downtown gambling halls where the focus was on gaming. Hull wanted his guests to feel like they were on vacation and having the time of their lives. He hoped they would go home and tell their neighbors and friends, who would want to vacation at the El Rancho Vegas as well.

The Western motif was extended to the staff. Everyone, it seems, wore western outfits. Hull stopped wearing his customary tuxedo and could be seen greeting and talking to guests in jeans, a western shirt, and a ten-gallon hat.

Tommy Hull, at left, and orchestra leader Garwood Van. Image courtesy of UNLV's Special Collections.

The Garwood Van Orchestra would go out to the airport to greet customers and ensure that they got to the hotel safely. Bass player Guy Landis recalled, "Our very format was that 'the first impression is a lasting one.' That's why they were flamboyant days. I played off about seven thousand airplanes." (*Las Vegas Sun Sunday Magazine*, April 1, 1979)

For arriving flights, "we had a bass and accordion screamin' like gangbusters! And with one hand we would be shakin' hands. We wore guns, we were all cowboys." Landis recalled. "You could see their faces light up when they came off the plane and heard all the music; it made them feel important." (*Las Vegas Sun Sunday Magazine*, April 1, 1979)

Hull used his Hollywood connections to bring some of the best entertainment of the day to the El Rancho. Over the years, Sophie Tucker, the Last of the Red Hot Mamas and a favorite of Frank Sinatra's, became a mainstay at the El Rancho Vegas. It became popular for other entertainers to visit while Sophie Tucker or Joe E. Lewis were in town and join them on stage. Tucker often flew in for impromptu gigs with Lewis. This kept the showroom jumping until dawn.

Entertainers such as Peggy Lee, Zero Mostel, Guy Lombardo, Milton Berle, Buddy Hackett, Jackie Gleason, Jimmy Durante, Nat King Cole, Jerry Lewis and Dean Martin, Eartha Kitt, Kay Starr, Sammy Davis, Jr. with the Will Mastin Trio, the Williams Brothers, and the Ritz Brothers all played the showroom at the El Rancho Vegas.

The Chuckwagon Buffet was born at the El Rancho. Late at night, gamblers would get hungry, but they wouldn't want to break away from the tables to go to the dining room for a meal. Hull and Van devised the Chuckwagon Buffet, where those busy gambling could grab a quick sandwich and eat while trying their hand with Lady Luck.

The El Rancho was so successful that businessman R. E. Griffiths decided that there was enough room and clientele for two resorts. When he built the Hotel Last Frontier, he closely followed the model that Hull had perfected at the El Rancho Vegas.

The opening of the Hotel Last Frontier and the Flamingo Hotel spurred new growth on the Las Vegas Strip and Tommy Hull began to feel that perhaps the time had come for him to sell. He lived in Los Angeles and would commute to Las Vegas on a regular basis. After talking with his auditor, he sold the property to Joe Drown, who was an associate of Conrad Hilton's. The property passed through several hands, including Wilbur Clark's, before Maurice Katleman bought the property in 1947. His nephew, Beldon, inherited the property shortly after the sale.

Beldon Katleman, wanting a more modern look for the hotel, had some ideas. He renamed the Round-Up Room. It became the Opera House Theater

The Justice of the Peace with newlyweds Joanne Woodward and Paul Newman. Image courtesy of Bo Boisvert.

and he expanded the Casino area. He added a French Provincial motif to the bungalows. In 1947, the El Rancho consisted of twenty-two buildings and 144 rooms (which included the military quarters).

The riding stables were in the back of the hotel and were very popular not only with the guests but the dancers as well.

Actors Paul Newman and Joanne Woodward ushered in the era of Las Vegas celebrity weddings by getting married at the El Rancho Vegas on January 29, 1958. They were not yet superstars and Katleman had to send a memo to the staff outlining what was needed to make the wedding a success. They were married in Katleman's bungalow.

Katleman brought in investors and quickly gained control of the hotel. Under his guidance, the hotel soared to its glory days as an entertainment and resort haven in the desert. By 1960, the property had sixty-nine buildings and 220 rooms.

All of that came to an end early in the morning of June 17, 1960. A fire broke out in the main building and quickly spread. The call came into the fire station at 4:50 a.m., and three engine companies, two pumpers, and the brand new $50,000 airplane crash truck responded to the call.

By the time the trucks arrived, the main building of the hotel was engulfed in flames. They used over 30,000 gallons of water trying to fight the fire. Unfortunately, the fire eventually toppled the famed neon landmark sign, the Windmill.

The fire had begun in the back of the Opera House Theater, but it had gotten hot and out of control very quickly. The evacuation of the theater, the casino, and the shops, surprisingly enough, was very orderly.

The El Rancho on fire. Image
courtesy of Bo Boisvert.

The smoke from the fire was so thick that entertainers Pearl Bailey, Mimi
Hines, and her husband, Phil Ford, jumped into Bailey's car and backed into a
tree trying to leave the hotel. Betty Grable and her husband, Harry James, had
been performing a late show in the Opera House Theater and lost over $10,000
in costumes. Grable was seen crying openly while watching the fire. Comedian
Red Skelton was photographed taking home movies of the tragic fire.

The next morning, Katleman displayed a mass of metal that had been silver
dollars. Over $400,000 in silver dollars and other coins were lost during the fire.
However, Sheriff Butch Leypoldt and his undersheriff, Lloyd Bell, had pried
open the vault with a crowbar and were responsible for saving boxes of money.

In less than an hour, the first resort that had started the famed Las Vegas
Strip was gone.

Katleman promised to rebuild an even bigger and grander El Rancho Vegas
but that never happened. It became a motel operation that only served to remind
the old-timers of what a wonderful place it had been. Katleman put the property
up for sale in the late 1960s. Howard Hughes bought the property for $7.5
million. Hughes put down $2.7 million in earnest money and the rest in an
escrow account. Before the deal could be finalized, Katleman demanded more
money. Hughes balked and the two went to court for over two years.

Finally, they settled out of court with Hughes paying Katleman an extra million dollars. Instead of doing anything with the property, Hughes just let the remaining buildings and bungalows bake in the desert sun. Some of the buildings were trucked out to Henderson and became part of the Old Vegas theme park, which in turn became Westworld, another unsuccessful theme park, and is now a housing development.

When I was a teenager growing up in Las Vegas, you could still see some of the bungalows on the property and follow the driveways around to long gone destinations. One morning, we woke up and the bungalows had been moved off the property and the remaining buildings were demolished.

Where are the bungalows today? As of this writing, one is privately owned and was relocated to Pahrump, one is on E. Charleston Blvd near the Ralph Jones Display Company, and another is an Antique Store also on East Charleston.

In the 1980s, the Hughes Corporation sold the property to the Bennett family, then owners of the Sahara Hotel. They, like Hughes before them, did nothing with the property. In 2007, the Bennett family sold the property to a developer.

What will be built on the land that once housed the first dude ranch resort on the Las Vegas Strip? Today, the land is being used for music festivals. Will another hotel be built there?

Only time will tell.

Author's note: The El Rancho Vegas has no connection other than a similar name to the newer El Rancho which was built on the old Thunderbird property back in the 1980s.

Menu cover for the El Rancho Vegas. Image courtesy of UNLV's Special Collections.

3

THE HOTEL LAST FRONTIER
1942-2007

A WESTERN DREAM REALIZED

In 1941, wealthy theater magnate R. E. Griffith, and his nephew, architect William J. Moore, were passing through Las Vegas on their way to California to purchase building materials for a resort they were planning in Deming, New Mexico. There wasn't much to see along the bumpy two-lane black-top highway besides tumbleweeds and the occasional billboard. As they drew nearer, they could see the El Rancho Vegas under construction. As they passed the occasional small saloon and Guy McAfee's 91 Club, the only major building was Tommy Hull's resort hotel rising out of the desert floor like a mirage.

They were struck with an idea.

"We came to Las Vegas and found that the opportunities were fabulous." Moore recounted in his oral history. (William Moore Oral History, *The Pioneer Tapes, 1981*, UNLV Special Collections)

They scrapped their plans for the resort in Deming and decided to build on property just south of the El Rancho Vegas. Griffith and Moore decided if they built south of the El Rancho Vegas, travelers on the LA Highway (Highway 91) would see their resort first and be tempted to pull in to their resort instead of the El Rancho Vegas. They took an interest in the 91 Club and tracked down Guy McAfee, the owner of the property. They negotiated a price and for $35,000 bought thirty-five acres of highway-fronted property. McAfee was overjoyed to have sold the land for so much money, thinking he had suckered a couple of rubes into overpaying for the property. Moore and his colleague, Jack Corgan, did the final drawings for the resort in a hotel room in Dallas.

As the El Rancho was nearing completion, Moore moved to Las Vegas to oversee construction of the Hotel Last Frontier. From the beginning, Griffith and Moore set out to make their hotel the favorite destination of tourists.

The Hotel Last Frontier. Image courtesy of the Nevada State Museum, Las Vegas.

Las Vegas architects Walter Zick and Harrison Sharp created this rendering of the Hotel Last Frontier. Image courtesy of As We Knew It: Classic Las Vegas Collection.

Despite the remote location and the jeers from people in town, the Hotel Last Frontier began to take shape. Unfortunately for Griffith and Moore, they were building their resort while World War II was raging. On the home front, rationing was the law of the day.

"They exempted anybody that had started construction ... providing they could prove that they had the material before the institution of the War Production Board," Moore said in an extensive interview that became his oral history. (William Moore Oral History, *The Pioneer Tapes, 1981*, UNLV Special Collections)

Moore's group proved it, but then ran into a catch: The Board also had authority to seize materials for the war effort. By listing the materials they had to complete construction, they also provided the government a list of what was available to commandeer.

> They did come to us while we were under construction and asked us to prove the existence of these materials and so forth. We had no alternative but to prove it if we wanted to continue with construction. But naturally, in proving it, gave the government a list of everything that you had. So they came in on our construction job at the hotel and essentially grabbed all of the material we had having to do with anything electrical and took the material in trucks to the Army air base at Nellis.
>
> William Moore Oral History, *The Pioneer Tapes, 1981*,
> UNLV Special Collections

The rationing forced Moore to get creative. He went to northern Nevada and bought two mines in Pioche, so that the construction crew could strip it of all the wiring, conduit, and switches, and then had it all shipped to the construction site.

> We were up against the problem of continuing the operation. We sent a crew up there to strip the material out of the mines: wiring, casing, pipe, major control switches, even small switches. We had brought an electrician out of Gallup, New Mexico, to run the electrical end of this business. His suggestion was that if we could find a couple of underground operations where they had been forced to run electrical supply lines and so forth, that there would be enough major electrical equipment, including wire and conduit, that we could obtain the exemptions against the code and go ahead and be able to finish the operations, Moore explained.
>
> William Moore Oral History, *The Pioneer Tapes, 1981*,
> UNLV Special Collections

To avoid further government scrutiny, all parties agreed to keep the sale on the down low. Moore also did not disclose the purchase of two ranches in Moapa Valley that would provide the hotel clientele with fresh eggs, chicken, and beef.

> Once we converted [the ranches] into a dairy with 300 milk cows and bought most of the milk [products]. [We got our herd] out of Cache Valley, Utah. [We] made our own butter, were able to make our own buttermilk. Got our own milk, you might say, in a much more desirable form and fresher than you would've been able to get out of the local dairy. We later took the second ranch, which we had set up as a dude ranch in the beginning, and converted it into registered cattle and the growing of cattle for butchering for the hotel. We were able to obtain permits for the rest, so that essentially we were able to sell the cattle to processors, who turned around and sold the meat back to us. … When it got up to the point that we didn't have any points and we couldn't make a trade with the Army or Navy at Nellis, then we just sold the cattle to the processors, who in turn were able to furnish us with enough stamps to make our own cattle purchases back.
>
> William Moore Oral History, *The Pioneer Tapes, 1981*,
> UNLV Special Collections

Despite the wartime rationing, they brought the finest stonemasons and Native Americans from the Ute tribe in New Mexico in by bus to lay the stonework for the fireplaces and patios. They also hired expert silversmiths and saddle makers to craft saddles and other finery for the hotel's bar and lobby.

Unlike the sprawling exterior of the El Rancho Vegas, the Hotel Last Frontier was modeled more like a traditional hotel, albeit western style:

> The main building was in the form of a U. The part [with] the rooms was in the form of an old fort—in other words, completely enclosed on four sides with entrances under the second floor back into the center section, which was highly landscaped in a western-type character. There was an outside boiler room or machinery room that housed most of the major machinery for the operation. Other than house the boilers, it housed the major air conditioning equipment. We used cold water circulated in tunnels under the hotel to cool, with an individual unit in each room.
>
> William Moore Oral History, *The Pioneer Tapes, 1981*,
> UNLV Special Collections

The lobby portion was the tallest, with a broad shingled roof and a porch stretching across its front. It was made principally of stone blocks with a huge double fireplace as the center of interest:

The hotel's motto was "the early west in modern splendor." Image courtesy of the Nevada State Museum, Las Vegas.

The ceilings were of hewn timbers—logs—rough-sawed boards antiqued in such a way as to look many years older. And the whole structure was laid out on that basis. The stone came from Red Rock Canyon, but the installation of same was made principally by Navajo Indians that we were able to bring in from Gallup, New Mexico.

William Moore Oral History, *The Pioneer Tapes, 1981,*
UNLV Special Collections

"They had the prettiest lobby you'd ever want to see. There was big old five-sided fireplace in there and the floor was like sandstone," remembered Merle Richards, then the owner of the Little Chapel of the West. (*Las Vegas Sun Sunday Magazine*, April 8, 1979).

The balcony leading from the lobby had a stairway made from split logs. The terrace was surrounded by the wagon wheels:

A fellow by the name of Gibbs [*author's note: Gibbs also provided the mules for the famed Borax 20-Mule Team*], was, you might say, a teamster in Las Vegas. He actually was in the business of plowing up land with horse-drawn equipment because the horse could get into spots the big tractor couldn't. He happened to have horses, and he didn't own tractors. Over a period of years he had been in this business to the extent that he had wagons break down, and people would come to him wanting to sell him wheels and so forth. In view of the fact that there were so few people around that were interested in purchasing such stuff, he acquired most of this stuff very cheap. That being the case, he had an awful lot of equipment in the way of wagon wheels, horse-drawn harnesses, that is a harness for horses on horse-drawn vehicles, and anything to do with a horse in the form of construction equipment. Through Gibbs, we were able to purchase most of the wagon wheels and other stuff.

William Moore Oral History, *The Pioneer Tapes, 1981*,
UNLV Special Collections

The resort's main show and dining room, the Ramona Room, continued the western theme with flagstone and large wooden beams. The stage had a wooden shake roof with big logs to support it out over the dance floor. There was seating enough for six hundred guests. (*Las Vegas Sun Sunday Magazine,* April 8, 1979)

South of the Ramona Room was the cocktail lounge, The Carrillo Room. The Carrillo Room was faced in stone and had French doors that led out onto a patio ringed in wagon wheels. Named for Leo Carrillo, a well-known actor who had co-starred in *Viva Villa!* and who would be beloved for his role as Pancho, the Cisco Kid's sidekick in the television series, the room featured a large painting of Carrillo astride his horse. The room also included the original octagonal tower that had been part of the 91 Club.

The interior of the Ramona Room. Image courtesy of the J. Florian Mitchell Collection, Nevada State Museum, Las Vegas.

Mr. Griffith, due to having operated a theater a number of years, knew and had made friends with many performers in the theater-film industry. He knew and was a very good friend of Leo Carrillo, who was known at that particular time as quite a western star. He got a hold of Mr. Carrillo, asked him to come to Las Vegas [and] asked for permission on the telephone to name a room after him, which essentially was a bar. Essentially the Pair-O-Dice Club was made up of a bar and a casino. We had a make-believe fireplace built into the bar. And we took out the dining room, naturally. We made restrooms and storage rooms out of a part of the space in the kitchen, and we used the other portion with the bar and the extension of the dining room as the Leo Carrillo Bar and had a picture of Leo Carrillo as a part of the decoration in the room, a very large picture.

William Moore Oral History, *The Pioneer Tapes*, 1981,
UNLV Special Collections

Raising eyebrows all around town, Moore bought the 40-foot-long, solid mahogany bar that had been the centerpiece for as long as locals could remember, at least, of the old Arizona Club on Block 16 in downtown Las Vegas. With the military wanting to open bases around the Valley, the businesses in the much-storied red-light district were in the process of being shuttered for good. Thus, the beautiful bar that had anchored the Arizona Club for years was moved to its new home.

The other bar was called the Gay '90s. [It] was the bar out of the old Arizona Club, which was in Block 16 of the red light district right in the heart of Las Vegas when I arrived in Las Vegas. We purchased the bar and the front entrance to the bar, which happened to be in the form of leaded glass, and put it into the hotel as the Gay '90s Bar, used it exactly as it was originally built other than the fact that we did add some saddle bar stools made out of leather in the form of a western saddle. Naturally, we had to make it comfortable. We didn't use the complete saddle design, but looking at the rear of the barstool was like looking at the rear of a saddle. So in some cases, there were stools big enough for two people because you would actually be seated on the side of the saddle.

William Moore Oral History, *The Pioneer Tapes, 1981*,
UNLV Special Collections

Knowing water was a necessity in the desert, Moore had a deep well drilled and almost a mile of tunnels were dug at the hotel to lay utility pipes. A large water tank was erected for storage. For fire protection, hose boxes were installed every 50 feet inside and outside the building. There was a 238-foot sun deck leading

Guests arriving by stagecoach at the Hotel Last Frontier. Image courtesy of UNLV's Special Collections.

from the second-floor rooms on the North Wing. Rooms from the West Wing led onto a small porch, which had stairs going down to the area where a 250-foot patio garden was planted. Badminton and tennis courts were under construction. It was reported that 3,700 trees, plants, and shrubs were placed around the grounds.

Stagecoaches picked up guests at the airport. Pack trips could be arranged and a riding stable, that also rented horses by the hour for those who wanted to go riding, was toward the back of the property.

The gift shop was owned by Moore's sister and contained unusual Indian and Mexican jewelry, as well as western costumes for both men and women.

[The gift shop sold] all types of western jewelry, Indian jewelry, turquoise, silver, even down to gold and whatnot. But there was more turquoise and silver than gold items. Then they sold saddles; they sold bridles. There was one silver-mounted saddle and bridle there that was worth thousands of dollars that they did sell to somebody out of that gift shop. Who they sold to, I don't remember.

William Moore Oral History, *The Pioneer Tapes, 1981*,
UNLV Special Collections

The guest rooms had furniture specially designed. The beds had head and foot-boards of dyed saddle leather, and window valances and mirror frames to match.

In 1979, Merle Richards, who had been the owner of the Little Church of the West wedding chapel, remembered, "Everything was western. The beds had horns over them and there were cow horns everywhere. The headboards looked like big oxen yokes and the chandeliers looked like they came off a ranch. If they had left it that way it would be beautiful today." (*Las Vegas Sun Sunday Magazine*, April 8, 1979)

The pool, while small, no doubt, by today's standards, was situated right out front where tourists from southern California, tired and hot from the multi-hour drive, could see the shimmering turquoise water as they drove closer. It also helped that bevy of pretty young ladies were either sitting poolside or playing in the pool.

The resort rivaled, in spirit, the great rustic national park resorts of the West—Yellowstone's Old Faithful Inn by Robert Reamer, Yosemite's the Ahwanee by Gilbert Stanley Underwood, and the Grand Canyon's Bright Angel Lodge by Mary Colter.

The hotel opened on October 30, 1942. The grand opening of the Last Frontier honored officers from the Army Air Corps Gunnery School located north of Las Vegas and military camps in California and Arizona, and funds were raised to benefit army recreation centers and camps. Griffith died within a year of the resort's opening, and Moore was named the Vice-President and General Manager.

The 600-seat Ramona Room was the Showroom and Griffith and Moore called upon the connections they had made in the theater business to fill the room with entertainment. Maxine Lewis, who had started as a dancer and was the Entertainment Director for the El Rancho Vegas, soon left there and took the same job at the Hotel Last Frontier.

I'll never forget opening night, all the town's leading citizens attended, stepping over the rugs as the carpet men were putting down the last tacks. I also will never forget the crowd shaking their heads and saying it would never be a success as the hotel was too big and plushy for Las Vegas.

My show budget at that time was $1,000 for three acts. Advertising for the show consisted of just two pictures of the stars, and they were always dressed in Western style. The ads I ran in the *Hollywood Reporter* and *Daily Variety* consisted of the hotel personnel on horseback going for the mail and all sorts of gimmicks such as meeting guests at the train or plane with a stage coach or any other Western vehicle I would find.

Maxine Lewis Oral History, 1987, UNLV Special Collections

Maxine Lewis was one of the first female entertainment directors on the Las Vegas Strip. Image courtesy of the J. Florian Mitchell Collection, Nevada State Museum, Las Vegas.

In 1944, Lewis contacted Sophie Tucker and signed her to play the fledgling resort (until El Rancho Vegas owner Tommy Hull stole her away). The Last of the Red Hot Mamas had no idea where Las Vegas was when she agreed to perform. She arrived at the Union Pacific train depot at the west end of Fremont Street where she was met by Lewis and the local fire chief. She rode to the Hotel Last Frontier in style, on the back of the hook and ladder truck.

Maxine Lewis soon made another entertainment coup. She had heard about a young pianist who was connecting with audiences wherever he played. Though currently performing at the Mount Royal Hotel in Montreal, she made the international call and asked to speak with Walter Liberace. When Liberace came on the line, Lewis got straight to the heart of the matter. She asked him if he would be interested in playing Las Vegas? He replied he was. She then asked him how much he was currently making.

Liberace stretched the truth and told her he was making $750 a week. In reality, he was making $350, but Lewis agreed to pay him $750 per week.

Since Liberace obviously had good business acumen, he sized up his first-night audience, and decided to delete several of the classical pieces, concentrating on boogie-woogie and popular tunes. The audience went wild, and Maxine Lewis called him to her office, where she tore up the $750-per-week contract and gave him a new one for $1,500. Later, he would sign a ten-year contract with the hotel at an even higher salary. (K. J. Evans, *The First 100*)

By most accounts, Moore was a promoter. He began junkets, first by bus, then later by plane, often using an up and coming entrepreneur, Kirk Kerkorian's chartered air service, to entice Californians to visit the resort. Sunday afternoons were scheduled with rodeos and roping contests.

As the El Rancho had popularized the late-night/early morning Chuckwagon Buffet for gamblers and those who were fans of the lounge performers, the Hotel Last Frontier popularized the Sunday morning brunch with its Hunt Breakfast. Moore also hired a woman, Helen Connors, as his administrative assistant and she became one of the first women in the hotel industry to hold that position.

Moore proved himself very adept at the business of running the Hotel Last Frontier. He was elected twice as the President of the Chamber of Commerce. His reputation for honesty so impressed Governor Vail Pittman that Pittman named Moore to the Nevada State Tax Commission despite Moore's involvement with gaming. The Nevada State Tax Commission would be the forerunner of licensing casino owners in Nevada. In 1950, Moore was a principal witness in the Kefauver Crime Committee hearings in Las Vegas.

To accommodate the growing number of tourists coming by auto, a Texaco gas station was created as an 1856 fire house which was operated by William "Andy" Anderson. On display was a hand-pulled fire engine. The carriage was supported by four large wood-spoke wheels and had a revolving drum in the center of wood, brass, and nickel. What attracted the greatest number of visitors was the brilliant neon sign over the gas station canopy. It depicted horses drawing a pumper, even to smoke belching from the stack, with two firemen aboard.

(The gas station) was designed by [Walter] Zick and [Harris] Sharp, Las Vegas architects. Originally, because Texaco [had] been using a fire chief—old, you might say, western-type advertising on their stations and promotion—we felt that it was a good tie-in with the old fire engine and tied in with Texaco's advertising. … Part of the idea was to put showers, restrooms, and so forth that would be inducive [*sic*] to the people cleaning up after a drive across the desert. The restrooms were rather elaborate—quite a number of stools and lavatories—various types of equipment that we could use in promotion, where the people would have the service that could be advertised on the road.
William Moore Oral History, *The Pioneer Tapes, 1981,*
UNLV Special Collections

The Texaco Station was designed to fit into the surroundings of the Hotel Last Frontier. Image courtesy of the Nevada State Museum, Las Vegas.

From the beginning, Griffith and Moore had envisioned their resort as "the early west in modern splendor" and that included an old pioneer town, called the Last Frontier Village.

In 1947, Moore began working with a well-connected local, Robert F. Caudill, better known around town as "Doby Doc." Caudill had gotten his nickname from one of his various businesses, The Adobe Doctor. He and Moore went over the layout of the Village. Caudill began the arduous task of filling the Village with authentic props. By the time Caudill was finished acquiring all the props from ghost towns around the state and by other means, he had almost 900 tons of Old West memorabilia. (Jeff Burbank, *Online Nevada*)

Props included a Joss House (that Caudill had gotten in Elko)—a small temple built for Chinese railroad workers in the 1860s and said to be the oldest surviving one in the United States. (It is now in storage at the Nevada State Museum, Las Vegas.) It held a hand carved, gold leaf teak wood shrine with tapestries said to be from the Ming Dynasty.

A wooden jail that served Tuscarora in the 1870s still had its interior walls equipped with leg irons, and was charred by an escape-by-fire plot, which went awry and burned to death the man trying to escape. There were real prairie

Robert "Doby Doc" Caudill.
Image courtesy of the J. Florian
Mitchell Collection, Nevada
State Museum, Las Vegas.

schooners as well as real old-fashioned horse-drawn fire engines. It is not known if Moore and/or the management of the Hotel Last Frontier knew the various, somewhat dubious methods that Caudill used to acquire many of his antiques. (A. D. Hopkins, *The First 100*)

According to Moore the freight bill that Caudill submitted for payment was for $37,000 and that was in pre-1950 dollars! (*Las Vegas Sun Sunday Magazine*, April 8, 1979).

The Last Frontier Village was a mix of museum pieces and retail establishments and there was a complete railroad train and tracks. According to Paul Ralli, a local attorney who wrote about his days in Las Vegas in *Viva Vegas*, the Village included "a drug store, general store, post office, schoolhouse and jail," as well as the "original printing plant of the venerable *Reese River Reveille*, Nevada's oldest newspaper." There was also a beauty parlor, a museum, athletic club, and kiddie arcade.

In addition to the items he traveled the state collecting, "Doby Doc" had a private collection of guns and other historic items. Moore convinced him to put his private collection on display as well. The Last Frontier Village opened in 1950 and some say it was an inspiration for Walt Disney's original Frontierland when Disneyland opened in 1955 in Anaheim, California.

Concept drawing of Last Frontier Village by architect Richard Stadelman. Image courtesy of the Nevada State Museum, Las Vegas.

The Little Church of the West, one of the first wedding chapels on the Strip, had been located next to the Hotel Last Frontier since it had opened its doors in 1942. That changed in 1954, when it was moved to the Last Frontier Village. By the late 1970s, the land it sat on was slated to be developed for the Fashion Show Mall and the Church was moved to the Hacienda Hotel. In 1996, it moved across the famed boulevard to its current location opposite Mandalay Bay.

THE NEW FRONTIER

In 1950, Moore announced that the hotel had purchased an additional 42 acres and was undergoing a $1 million expansion program.

In 1951, the Golden Slipper Saloon and Gambling Hall opened as part of the Last Frontier Village. Guests were encouraged to wager via an antique Wheel of Fortune that had reportedly been used in nineteenth century mining camps. The Golden Slipper had the Flora-Dora Girls, a dance troupe in period costumes that performed nightly in the Old Bar.

Also in 1951, Moore ultimately decided that he needed a change and put the Hotel Last Frontier up for sale. Jake Kozloff, Beldon Katleman, and Guy McAfee

The *porte cochere* at the New Frontier Hotel. Image courtesy of the Nevada State Museum, Las Vegas.

The Silver Slipper was originally built as part of the Last Frontier Village. Image courtesy of the Nevada State Museum, Las Vegas.

bought the property for $5.5 million. Moore would take his profits and become involved in both the El Cortez in downtown Las Vegas and the Showboat Hotel out on Boulder Highway, then the main thoroughfare for traffic from Utah and Arizona.

Kozloff had visited Las Vegas in 1946 and become friends with Guy McAfee. McAfee, of course, had taken the money he made selling the 91 Club to R. E. Griffith back in 1941 and had gone down to Fremont Street where he invested in the Golden Nugget and was doing quite well. Kozloff was soon invited to join the management staff of the Nugget. From there, he began to eye larger properties like the Hotel Last Frontier.

The Hotel Last Frontier sale included the casino/hotel property, the Last Frontier Village and the Silver (formerly the Golden) Slipper Gambling Hall and Saloon. Kozloff was named president of the hotel and his younger brother, Bill, became his administrative assistant.

The new owners, however, sensed that America's tastes were changing and refurbished the hotel into more of a mid-century space age theme and away from the original western theme. The ad slogan was changed from "The Early West in Modern Splendor" to "The New Frontier: Out of this World."

They quickly realized that they would have to get creative in order to successfully re-theme the hotel. Instead of closing the Hotel Last Frontier, they built the New Frontier just north of the original. The New Frontier would be a

The New Frontier and its mid-century modern splendor. Photo courtesy of the Nevada State Museum, Las Vegas.

two-story building with balconies on the second floor and a *porte cochere* that welcomed auto drivers off the highway. The front lawn of the Hotel Last Frontier was paved over as a parking lot—it's the Vegas way after all. The new pool was built in the rear of the building.

Because of construction for the New Frontier buildings, the Little Church of the West was moved to the south end of the property closer to the Silver Slipper and Last Frontier Village. The Last Frontier continued to operate while construction continued on the new hotel.

In February 1954, actor Ronald Reagan graced the stage of the original hotel's showroom, the Ramona Room, in a short-lived career as a night club performer. For $15,000 a week for four weeks, Reagan hosted, told stories, sang with a singing group called the Continentals and even performed with trained chimpanzees. The Blackburn Twins and Evelyn Ward and the Honey Brothers completed the bill. By most accounts, Reagan was a serviceable, if not memorable performer. Shortly thereafter, Reagan returned to Hollywood to host *The General Electric Theater* and continue his interest in politics.

In April, a group of buyers that included Murray Randolph, a real estate executive from Los Angeles, Irv Leff, a Los Angeles businessman, and Maurice Friedman, purchased Kozloff's and McAfee's interest in the hotel.

Ronald Reagan, with his name on the marquee, and friends at the Hotel Last Frontier. Image courtesy of the Nevada State Museum, Las Vegas.

Friedman explained the musical chairs of ownership to George Stamos in a 1979 interview, "A group of buyers that included Murray Randolph, Irving Leff and myself purchased the Last Frontier, which was already being converted into the New Frontier, from Jake Kozloff and Guy McAfee." (*Las Vegas Sun Sunday Magazine*, April 8, 1979).

Meanwhile construction continued on the new building. The lobby of the New Frontier was done in charcoal gray with white and pink leather sofas with chrome, aluminum, and a color scheme that included deep blues, reds, and purples. A mural depicted alien space men heading toward the casino. The Cloud 9 Cocktail Lounge had a mural of celestial objects including flying saucers and was reputed to have the longest bar in the world. The chandeliers in the casino were also shaped like spacecraft.

The Coffee Shop was called the Planet Room and the showroom was dubbed the Venus Room.

The Venus Room was built to accommodate seating for 808 with twelve horse-shoe-style tiers making the showroom a large amphitheater. For the late show, it could hold 972 people. The stage was 38 feet in diameter with a revolving stage 30 feet in diameter, and two side stages. The orchestra was on a hydraulic lift, the first in town, so that the musicians wouldn't obscure the view of the audience.

The pylon sign for the New Frontier rose 126 feet in the night sky and pulsated with multi-colored lights inside the inverted stacked cones. The hotel's outer

Guests enjoy the show at the New Frontier Hotel. Image courtesy of the J. Florian Mitchell Collection, Nevada State Museum, Las Vegas.

façade featured a 70-foot-long *porte cochere* that swept out over the entrance into a curl. It was a mid-century modern marvel that paid homage to the Atomic Age, though, locals were reportedly sad to see the original buildings replaced with such different architecture. (*Las Vegas Sun Sunday Magazine*, April 8, 1979)

On September 21, 1954, the Nevada Tax Commission ordered a full-scale hearing at its October session into the tangled financial affairs of the resort. One action filed by Beldon Katleman accused the remaining licensees at the hotel of mismanagement and selling undisclosed interests in the casino in violation of state gambling laws. Katleman, who owned nineteen percent of the hotel, filed a $1 million action against Jake Kozloff, his brother William Kozloff, and Murray Randolph. Katleman, and the three men were the only licensees listed to operate the gambling at the resort.

The New Frontier officially opened on April 4, 1955. International recording star and actor, Mario Lanza, was to open the new Venus Showroom. Unfortunately, Lanza, according to various sources, went on a bender and was unable to sing that night. Ray Bolger, Jimmy Durante, and Gisele MacKenzie, among others, stepped in to keep the evening from being a complete disaster. Lanza left town shortly thereafter and the performers continued for the run of his contract.

On the southern end of the property, the Frontier Sports Drome was built behind the resort. The Sports Drome was the home to the Nevada Racing Association and every other week, fifty-two stock cars would take to the track for a 105-lap race that was popular with tourists and locals alike.

The musical chairs ownership continued. In 1956, the hotel was leased to German munitions heiress Vera Krupp, Louis Manchon, and Sidney Bliss. Krupp and her partners didn't see eye to eye and they lost money. In order to avoid being sued, Krupp returned the property to the 1954 owners (Randolph, Leff, and Friedman) on St. Patrick's Day, 1957. The casino was closed down and the hotel was operated as a motel until December of 1957, while they searched for a casino operator suitable for licensing.

In April 1956, Colonel Tom Parker signed a contract for Elvis Presley to appear in the Venus Room for a two-week run. Comedian Shecky Greene would be the opening act, Elvis Presley—billed as "the Atomic Powered Singer"—was the second act, and the main act was Freddy Martin and his Orchestra.

A *Las Vegas Sun* staff writer wrote two days before the opening,

Elvis Presley, unanimously acclaimed by critics as the most important singing find since Johnnie Ray, will open in the New Frontier Hotel's, Venus Room Monday, April 23, as a special added attraction to the Freddy Martin show.

Elvis Presley played the New Frontier
Hotel and bombed. Image courtesy of
the Nevada State Museum, Las Vegas.

The young vocalist will be featured in one of the most lavish productions ever
presented in the Venus Room, Lewis stated. Freddy Martin and his band, comic
Shecky Greene, the Venus Starlets and a cast of more than 60 performers will
make up the entertainment package.

Las Vegas Sun, April 21, 1956

Presley and his band were met with light applause but none of the wild enthu-
siasm and screaming that was more customary at their appearances. The overall
reaction to the young Presley was less than stellar. The tourists who came to
Las Vegas in 1956 were not the up and coming rock and roll crowd but an older
crowd who preferred Tin Pan Alley hits and singers.

Bill Willard wrote in his review of the evening,

Elvis Presley, arriving here on the wave of tremendous publicity, fails to hit
the promised mark in a desert isle surfeited with rock and rollers who play
in shifts atop every cocktail lounge on the Strip. The brash, loud braying of
his rhythm and blues catalog (and mind you, they are big hits everywhere it
seems) which albeit rocketed him to the big time, is overbearing to a captive
audience. In a lounge, one can up and go fast. But in a dining room, the table
sitter must stay, look and listen the thing out. Which is perhaps why Presley

received applause on his opening show edged with polite inference only. For the teen-agers, the long, tall Memphis lad is a whiz; for the average Vegas spender or showgoer, a bore. His musical sound with a combo of three is uncouth, matching to a great extent the lyric content of his nonsensical songs.

Las Vegas Sun, April 28, 1956

To salvage the gig, Colonel Parker agreed that Presley would do a show just for the teenagers on the following Saturday. That appearance was packed with young fans that knew who Presley was and appreciated his music.

In a letter to the *Sun*, Las Vegas local Ed Jameson wrote regarding the less than stellar reviews the young singer had received:

Youth is an exuberant stage of life with the top down. Presley's voice is that of American youth looking at the moon and wondering how long it will take to get there. He is not a Rock 'n Roller nor is he a cowboy singer. He is something new coming over the horizon all by himself and he deserves his ever-growing audience. Nobody should miss him. Parents would do well to take their children to hear him. It would be a good way to get to know and understand your own kids.

Las Vegas Sun, May 12, 1956

A Travel Guide published in 1957 noted: "Tourists enjoy the Chuck Wagon suppers, served from ten in the evening till seven the next morning—price, $1.50—and breakfast is served twenty-four hours a day. Nowhere in the world is there anything quite like it—this informal magnificence at multi-million dollar hotels at little more than motel rates; and you can take your choice of nearly a dozen of the nation's top-flight shows for the price of a drink. Of course, the casinos carry the load."

In 1958, following the Late Show, at 4:30 a.m. on Sunday mornings, the Venus Room was used for Catholic Mass. The first Mass took place on Oct. 8, 1958. In attendance were Doc Bayley, actor Preston Foster and 127 employees ranging from dancers to pit bosses to *maitre d's*. The Mass helped spur interest in building a church on or near the Strip for hotel employees and performers. The Guardian Angel Church designed by famed African-American architect Paul Revere Williams would be built a few years later.

The hotel was still experiencing financial instability and the owners turned to an experienced operator to help them out. Warren "Doc" Bayley fit that bill. Bayley had opened the Hacienda Hotel on what was then the far reaches of the southern Strip in 1956. He took an interest in helping out the New Frontier. According to Friedman, "In his contract, Bayley had the option to buy the hotel

Warren "Doc" Bayley, owner of the Hacienda Hotel, took an interest in the New Frontier Hotel. Image courtesy of As We Knew It: Classic Las Vegas Collection.

but he remained our tenant until he died in December, 1964. When he died his rights went to Bankers Life, which exercised the purchase option that January." (*Las Vegas Sun Sunday Magazine*, April 8, 1979).

Richard Taylor, who was "Doc" Bayley's right-hand man at the Hacienda, was transferred over to the New Frontier to manage the hotel.

> Doc's most exciting idea was 30 years too early. At that time (1958) the word "condominium" was just beginning to appear in the business sections of the dailies. Many had a hard time pronouncing it. But Bayley caught the concept immediately and announced to his board of directors he wanted to build the world's largest hotel by selling 2,500 rooms to individuals under the new condominium idea.
>
> All he needed, he said, was 2,500 people to invest $10,000 each—the cost of constructing one room in those day—and he could accomplish his goal. Then the hotel would rent the rooms for the owners and send owners their income dividends quarterly. The fee to book and service the rooms would be reasonable as Bayley was only interested in owning the casino and profiting from it … not the rooms!
>
> A front-page story of the *Las Vegas Evening Journal* announced Bayley's team: Shields B. Craft, an owner/operator of a small feeder airline was to be the first vice president; and myself was to be the managing director.
>
> Richard Taylor, 2002 interview with the author

Well-known movie star Preston Foster was to be the greeter at the new New Frontier. Preston Foster was a well-known actor who had appeared in a number of films including *Annie Oakley* with Barbara Stanwyck and *My Friend Flicka*. His personality fit Bayley's method of operating. It didn't take long for trouble to surround the new operators. The New Frontier was in the center of the Strip and had an entirely different type of customer. It soon became evident that the type of employees here were different from those who worked at the more populist Hacienda. What the Hacienda had developed out at the far end of the southern Strip so successfully could not be duplicated at the New Frontier Hotel.

Richard Taylor remembered,

> It was my responsibility to take some of the Hacienda's lifeblood (cash) from the Hacienda casino cage down to the New Frontier cage weekly ... sometimes daily ... when losses there could not be turned around. Even with the smash hit show (*Holiday in Japan*), we could not make any money. In fact, the cost of the show policy just exacerbated the problem. Even with well-known and respected casino executives like Eddie Hughes running the pit, we had a hard time paying our bills. Our purchasing agent Larry Rovere had his work cut out for him. He had to keep the hotel supplied while our bookkeeper Leonard Markson couldn't pay the bills.
>
> After almost two years of fighting an uphill battle, Bayley finally decided that the constant drain on the Hacienda finances was hurting the Hacienda and had to be stopped. The cost of rehabilitation of the old section of the hotel and installing a moving sidewalk to the adjoining operation we called "The Last Frontier" in memory of the original hotel, contributed to our problems.
>
> The town was shedding its image of the Old West and the "Last Frontier" failed badly. No one was interested in the past. The new and modern drew the customers as the Sahara and Riviera changed the scene in that part of the Strip.
>
> Richard Taylor in an interview with the author, 2002

The more things change, it seems, the more they stay the same.

In 1959, Bill Miller was brought in to be the Entertainment Director.

He quickly began to turn the entertainment around. The Treniers, one of the best rock and swing groups in the country, were hired. Francis Faye, Pete Barbutti, and bongo artist Jack Costanza were signed to contracts.

Claude Trenier remembered, "We'd begin at about midnight and play until 6:00 a.m., doing twenty- to thirty-minute sets." (Claude Trenier, interview with the author, 2003)

In 1960, the IRS seized the money from the Hotel Last Frontier and the New Frontier for unpaid taxes, and actor Preston Foster severed all ties with the Hotel.

Entertainment Director Bill Miller had owned his own nightclub in New Jersey before coming to Las Vegas. Image courtesy of the J. Florian Mitchell Collection, Nevada State Museum, Las Vegas.

THE FRONTIER HOTEL

In December 1964, "Doc" Bayley unexpectedly died, and the hotel came under the control of Banker's Life Insurance Company. They exercised the purchase option on the property that January.

John McArthur, the president of Banker's Life, kept the hotel closed for six months while he tried to find a tenant for the property. Unable to find a tenant, he asked Maurice Friedman to come back east to discuss the future. They decided the property needed more than just a makeover. McArthur authorized $6 million for the project. He wanted the original buildings torn down and construction began on a new 500-room hotel.

The Frontier Operating Company with Steve Wynn as one of the partners was formed and they took over the lease from Bankers Life in June 1967.

The new building was designed by Rissman and Rissman, a Los Angeles architectural firm, with 650 rooms and a new 186-foot tall sign designed by Bill Clark of Ad-Art. The sign contained more than a mile of fluorescent tubing, a mile and a half of neon and more than 23,000 light bulbs. The 30-foot tall *F* at the top of the sign rotated on a specially built mechanism. An enormous caisson was installed to keep the sign from toppling over in a Las Vegas windstorm.

The Frontier Hotel at night. Image courtesy of the Nevada State Museum, Las Vegas.

Burt Cohen was brought in to supervise the construction of the hotel. As part of his deal, he became part owner and was responsible for the hotel side of the business. This new hotel was built on the footprint of the original Hotel Last Frontier. The Last Frontier Village was closed and it was rumored that it would re-open with the new hotel. However, that did not happen. When the Village closed, it was forever. When he realized that the Village would not re-open as part of the new site, "Doby Doc" started dismantling it and began moving the wagons, stagecoaches, and larger props out to his homestead near the Tropicana Hotel.

Steve Wynn, barely twenty-five years old, invested $45,000 for a 3% share of the Frontier. He moved his family to Las Vegas and received his gaming license in June. Shortly afterward, he became the slot manager and assistant credit manager. When it came time to license the owners of the Frontier Operating Company, the owners hit a snag with the Licensing Board. Rumors swirled that one or more owners had connections to the mob. Wynn, apparently unaware of this, cashed out before convictions were handed down for concealing the true ownership of the hotel. Wynn learned a valuable lesson about business associates that he would carry with him in the years ahead.

Just before the hotel was set to open, Robert Maheu contacted the Frontier Operating Company on behalf of his employer, Howard Hughes. Hughes wanted to buy it before it opened for tax purposes. The thirty-five stockholders of the Frontier Operating Company refused Hughes' offer.

The latest version of the Frontier opened on July 20, 1967.

After the hotel opened and was operational, Hughes made another offer that included not only the Frontier property but the Silver Slipper Gambling Hall and Saloon property as well. This time the shareholders of the Frontier Operating Company accepted the deal. Hughes bought the property for $14 million.

The Nevada Gaming Commission accepted the purchase under "standard emergency regulations" that forced a midnight meeting of the commission to okay the purchase. Summa Corporation, the Hughes parent company, took control of the property.

Right away, Hughes decided that the New Frontier name had to go and rebranded the hotel just The Frontier. Hughes had bought the Silver Slipper because the revolving Slipper could be seen from his penthouse in the Desert Inn and he complained it kept him awake at night.

Wayne Newton, then billed as the Midnight Idol, signed a two-year contract with the Hotel. Newton was paid $50,000 a week. In a move that echoed his father's showbiz beginnings, Frank Sinatra, Jr., was performing at the hotel with Harry James.

On January 14, 1970, the Hotel hosted the final engagement of the 1960s popular Motown group, The Supremes. A live album called *Farewell* was recorded

The Silver Slipper sign kept Howard Hughes awake at night. Image courtesy of UNLV's Special Collections.

from the engagement, including the final night of the show. It was Diana Ross' last performance with the other two singers in the group, Mary Wilson and Cindy Birdsong. Guests such as Smokey Robinson, Dick Clark, Lou Rawls, Steve Allen, Johnny Carson, and Marvin Gaye, who attended the show, can be heard singing with Ross on the deluxe album. On May 7, 1970, Diana Ross returned to the stage of the Frontier as a solo performer with Sammy Shore (Pauly's dad) as her opening act.

During the 1970s, a number of employees who had once worked at the Frontier moved on to better jobs. Al Benedict, the food and beverage manager at the Last Frontier was working for Kirk Kerkorian; Joe Kelley, a former craps dealer at the hotel, became president of the Showboat; R. O. Cannon, a longtime Last Frontier manager, became general manager of the Union Plaza; and Bill Kozloff, an executive assistant for his older brother, Jake, became the vice president and general manager of the Four Queens.

In 1982, the Frontier managed to snag illusionists, Siegfried and Roy, away from *Donn Arden's Hallelujah Hollywood!* at the original MGM Grand Hotel. Siegfried and Roy's *Beyond Belief* set a new standard for showmanship as the entertainment landscape of the Strip began to shift from popular performers such as Frank Sinatra, Sammy Davis, Jr., and Liberace to magic and variety acts.

Show program for Siegfried and Roy's *Beyond Belief: An Amazing Spectacle*. Image courtesy of As We Knew It: Classic Las Vegas Collection.

In 1988, the Summa Corporation Hughes Company sold The Frontier to Margaret Elardi, the one-time owner of the Pioneer Club on Fremont Street. Elardi angered many long-time residents by tearing down the Silver Slipper for a parking lot — remember it's the Vegas way.

In September 1991, Elardi refused to come to an agreement with the powerful Culinary Union. The Culinary Union workers, citing cut hourly wages, decreasing benefits, and the elimination of contributions to the pension plan, called for a strike. Four other local unions—Bartenders 165, Teamsters 995, Operating Engineers 501, and Carpenters 1780 joined the striking Culinary workers. The showroom was closed until management and the unions could reach an agreement.

The strike lasted over six years and caused the Frontier to go into a steep decline as tourists refused to be caught in the middle between picketing workers and management.

In October 1997, Elardi sold the resort to Kansas businessman Phil Ruffin for $167 million. Ruffin settled with the Culinary Union and the long strike finally came to an end on January 31, 1998. The deal included a five-year contract and an additional $3.5 million for back wages owed to the striking workers.

Ruffin changed the name back to the New Frontier—though he kept the old sign that said The Frontier and set about trying to bring the hotel out of its decline.

Ruffin took an option on the 16.5-acre parking lot where the Silver Slipper had once stood. He forged a deal with Gilley's, the famous Texas bar and dance hall known for its mechanical bull-riding, and they opened a saloon in the New Frontier.

Over the years, he toyed with various ideas for revitalizing the hotel. In January 2000, Ruffin announced that he would close the New Frontier, implode the buildings and build a new hotel/casino themed around San Francisco and call it City by the Bay—never mind that there is no bay of water anywhere near the hotel site. It would feature replicas of such famous landmarks as the Golden Gate Bridge, Coit Tower, Chinatown, and Fisherman's Wharf. The main restaurant would be called Alcatraz and feature Napa Valley wines. He ambitiously hoped to have the new hotel/casino open for business by September 2002.

Casino designer Mark Advent who designed New York, New York filed a lawsuit against Ruffin. He claimed he had been working for two years with Ruffin on a San Francisco themed hotel. The plans, designs, and concepts were copyright protected by him and his company Advent Communications. Ruffin dismissed the complaint, saying, "city themes are in the public domain."

Ruffin ran into trouble financing the mega-resort and it was never built. The New Frontier was granted a reprieve from a date with bulldozers.

The Frontier Hotel got a new name and a makeover in the 1960s. Image courtesy of the Nevada State Museum, Las Vegas.

In January 2005, Donald Trump and Ruffin announced they were breaking ground on a sixty-four-floor condominium project that wasn't part of the hotel.

Ruffin said he planned to divest his hotels in the Bahamas and use that money to build a 3,000-room mega-resort/casino. This new resort would be called Montreux and be modeled after the Swiss resort town known for its jazz festivals. He planned to bring the Montreux Jazz Festival to his mega-resort as well. He also had plans for an observation wheel that would be in the front of the property, facing the Strip. It would be called the "Las Vegas Eye" and modeled after the famous one in London. Much to his consternation, he wasn't the only hotel owner thinking about a giant Ferris wheel.

But, like his City by the Bay mega-resort, the Montreux never got off the ground. The Frontier managed to elude the wrecking ball one more time.

In 2007, perhaps tired of all the uncertainty and with the land prices on the northern end of the Strip climbing higher into the stratosphere, Ruffin announced he had found a buyer for the property. The Elad Group bought the property (not including Trump Tower) for $1.2 billion and was ready to spend an additional $400 million to tear down the Frontier buildings and build the Las Vegas version of the famed Plaza Hotel in New York City. The Plaza would be a mixture of hotel and private luxury condos.

With that as the plan, the hotel closed forever on July 15, 2007. Ruffin, after saying he wouldn't, finally did offer 850 employees who stayed until the closing date severance packages based on their longevity with the hotel.

The offer included both union and non-union personnel. Those who had been with the hotel for twenty years or more received $8,000 with the scale declining for fewer years worked. The hotel and surrounding buildings were imploded on November 13, 2007.

The Elad Group ran into numerous problems including a battle over the use of the name Plaza with the owners of the Union Plaza on Fremont Street. Elad won that battle but the next one would deliver a body blow. The Great Recession hit and their grand plans to have the Plaza open by 2012 began to quickly fade.

The Trump Hotel opened on March 31, 2008.

The property that once housed the "early west in modern splendor" themed buildings, the Last Frontier Village, the mid-century modern marvel, The New Frontier, and the more generic Frontier Hotel buildings, the Silver Slipper and the Sports Drome, is still an empty lot more than eight years after its closing.

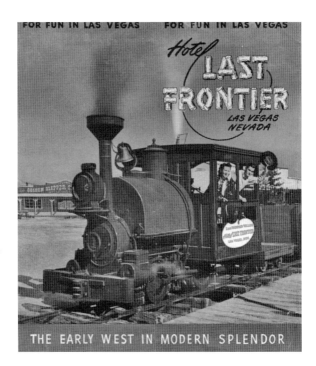

The Hotel Last Frontier played up its western theme in everything from brochures to menus. Image courtesy of UNLV's Special Collections.

4

THE FABULOUS FLAMINGO
1946-PRESENT

THE WILKERSON-SIEGEL YEARS

By now everyone has heard the myth. Benjamin Siegel—looking a great deal like movie star Warren Beatty—drives up a dusty highway into downtown Las Vegas. Not liking the dust, the desert rats drinking at the bar, or the frontier architecture, he gets in his car and heads back out of town. He pulls off the dusty, empty highway and has a fever dream. He announces to Virginia Hill, his driving companion–looking a great deal like actress Annette Bening—that here is where he will build the world's greatest hotel, The Fabulous Flamingo.

It's a pivotal moment in the film *Bugsy*, but the reality is that it is a myth.

Truth: The El Rancho Vegas and The Hotel Last Frontier were both doing good business on that same stretch of dusty highway before the Flamingo was even a thought.

Truth: The Flamingo Hotel was already under construction by the time Siegel joined the party. The hotel was the brainchild of Hollywood publisher and nightclub entrepreneur, Billy Wilkerson. Wilkerson published the *Hollywood Reporter* and owned a string of nightclubs in Los Angeles, including Ciro's, the Cafe Trocadero, and La Rue's, all popular with the Hollywood crowd. He also had a wicked gambling habit. Two of his friends, millionaire playboy Howard Hughes and movie mogul Joe Schenck, suggested that Wilkerson build a casino so he could "own" the house.

He saw the potential of what would become the famous Las Vegas Strip and wanting to be different from the other two hotels already doing business, he proposed a resort hotel that would draw the Hollywood crowd that he knew and catered to in Los Angeles. It would be a sophisticated carpet joint where the stars would want to come, play, and gamble.

In 1945, Wilkerson purchased 33 acres of property on the east side of Highway 91. He purchased the land from Margaret Folsom who had, in turn, purchased

The Fabulous Flamingo Hotel aglow at night. Image courtesy of the Nevada State Museum, Las Vegas.

the property from Las Vegas pioneers, Charles and Delphina Squires. Charles "Pop" Squires, who had come to the dusty railroad town in 1908 as a newspaper editor, was considered one of the founders of Las Vegas. "Pop" Squires had originally paid $288.75 for the property. Wilkerson paid $84,000 for the same 33 acres. On the site were two dilapidated shacks and motel sign that were crumbling into the desert sand.

The land was situated just a little further south than the other two existing hotels. The El Rancho Vegas and The Hotel Last Frontier were located on the west side of the highway, Wilkerson's resort would be the first one that tourists driving from southern California would see on the east side of the highway.

He hired the architect that had built Ciro's, George Vernon Russell, and interior designer, Tom Douglas. Wilkerson envisioned a casino, a Parisian-themed show-room, nightclub, athletic club, steam rooms, hotel rooms, and an award-winning restaurant that would hire European chefs. Wilkerson's other visionary idea was that the entire place would be air-conditioned. He also envisioned retail stores that would sell high-end jewelry and clothing, a suite of bungalows that would cater to his high-rolling guests, and a golf course.

The Flamingo Hotel under construction. Image courtesy of the Nevada State Museum, Las Vegas.

Wilkerson wanted his resort to be bigger than both of the other two hotels, so he planned for 250 rooms. The El Rancho Vegas at the time had 110 rooms and the Hotel Last Frontier had 107 rooms. He also wanted to break with the western theme of both the other two resorts and the casinos on Fremont Street. Wilkerson wanted a swanky place that would be considered classy for his high-end friends and gamblers. He was upping the ante towards the glitz and swank in a way that hadn't yet been seen by locals or travelers alike.

Myth: Siegel named the hotel The Flamingo after Virginia Hill's legs.

Truth: Wilkerson loved exotic birds and he adopted a tall, lanky pink bird as the logo for his new resort, The Flamingo.

It also was Billy Wilkerson who directed that there be no windows and no clocks on the walls in the casino. Being a gambler himself, he knew how they thought, and he knew how easy it was to lose track of time when gambling. His floor plan required that guests walk through the casino to get to the registration desk as well as the restaurants and the showroom.

With a budget of $1.2 million, construction began in November 1945. Wilkerson had a loan of $600,000 from Bank of America and another $200,000 from his

Hotel owner Billy Wilkerson loved flamingos. Image courtesy of UNLV's Special Collections.

friend Howard Hughes. Wilkerson took to playing craps in an attempt to win the remaining funds needed to build his dream resort. Unfortunately, Lady Luck was not riding with Billy Wilkerson that night. Instead of winning, he lost more than $200,000. Despondent over the loss, he—some would say foolishly—accepted an offer of $1 million from New York underworld figure, G. Harry Rothberg.

Rothberg's underworld partners included Meyer Lansky, Gus Greenbaum, Moe Sedway, and Lansky's childhood friend, Benjamin "Bugsy" Siegel. The partners had moved into Las Vegas gaming by muscling in on the local race wire that transmitted the results of horse races. They took the money made from that and bought, then quickly sold, the El Cortez for a $166,000 profit. They had been keeping an eye on Wilkerson's dream hotel and when Wilkerson crapped out at the tables, they made their move and became silent partners.

Wilkerson and Siegel had been friendly since the 1930s. They had gotten to know one another in Los Angeles, as Siegel was a frequent guest at Wilkerson's clubs, Ciro's and the Cafe Trocadero. Siegel very much wanted to break into the movies and hanging out with friends and stars at the nightclubs was one to garner attention in the trades. Since they already got along, Siegel and Wilkerson worked together overseeing the daily construction of the resort hotel. Wilkerson knew of Siegel's underworld ties and of his reputation. Siegel moved quickly to take over exclusive control of the property. Wilkerson agreed and Richard Stadelman, an architect from Los Angeles, was brought in, and Del Webb was hired to be the general contractor.

Resentments began to build and with Lansky's blessing, Siegel forced Wilkerson to give up creative control of the property and only remain as a shareholder. Wilkerson at the time owned 48% of the stock according to his son, W. R. Wilkerson. Siegel's first move was to fire Russell and Douglas and turn all of the architectural work over to Stadelman. In June 1946, Siegel formed the Nevada Projects Corporation and appointed himself president.

There was a housing shortage in post-war America and building materials were scarce and at a premium. Siegel did not have Bill Moore's and R. W. Griffith's creative thinking in dealing with the situation. Where Moore and Griffith had purchased mines and dairy farms, Siegel preferred to throw money at the problem. He went to San Francisco and somehow persuaded officials to let him have scarce building materials. This, in turn, caught the eye of the FBI and they secretly began to monitor Siegel's actions. The Feds were convinced that bribery had taken place.

Siegel continued to throw money at the materials shortage problem. He flew in carpenters and laborers and paid them top dollar. Not happy with the plans, he continued to make changes even after construction had begun. The boiler room and kitchen were rebuilt because he was unhappy with the final results. Long-time residents still talk about the profiteering that went on at the construction site.

He scaled back the number of rooms to ninety-three and wanted separate sewer lines for each room. He often bought material on the black market and paid top dollar for it. Because he kept making changes, the project was soon awash in $1 million worth of overruns. Siegel sold $1 million of stock in Nevada Corporations to Lansky, Wilkerson, and anyone who would buy in.

Siegel would buy the material and have it delivered only to have it stolen from the construction site. He would, unwittingly some believe, buy back the material once the theft had been discovered. Lansky and others came to believe that Siegel was behind the thefts and that more was going into Siegel's back pocket than was being spent on the Flamingo.

Siegel finally forced Billy Wilkerson to sign over his stock in the hotel, and Wilkerson fled to Paris. However, Billy Wilkerson did not give up so easily.

Siegel's Flamingo featured a trapshooting range, a nine-hole golf course, and tennis, squash, and badminton courts. The landscaping was lavish by Las Vegas standards of the day, and all the male staff were required to wear tuxedos. It was the most opulent hotel built and locals were eager to check out the new carpet joint. Siegel's attorney, Louis Wiener, said years later that Siegel's intention was to build a resort for the Hollywood crowd that included enough diversions so that when they lost at the tables they would still feel they were getting their money's worth.

The original Flamingo building followed the other two Strip resorts in its design. Eschewing flashy, the building was long in length but not multi-storied. That's where the similarities ended. The lines of the Flamingo were sleek and modern and the casino was asymmetrical and angled so that southbound traffic from downtown Las Vegas would see the main façade. The multi-storied hotel wings formed a horseshoe from the casino building, which protected the pool. The walls were reinforced concrete faced in green ashlar stone or stucco. (Alan Hess, *Viva Las Vegas: After-Hours Architecture*)

The hotel was landscaped by Stadelman to resemble an oasis with exotic plants and trees shipped from Los Angeles nurseries.

A pylon sign stood on top of the jutting canopy, over the casino building, advertising the name (the neon flamingo was added in 1947). An attraction board sign marked the driveway entrance to the hotel where the list of performers changed regularly. At the top of the marquee was a green neon clock designed by Hermon Beornge of the Young Electric Sign Company (YESCO for short).

The original sign and *porte cochere* at the Flamingo Hotel. Image courtesy of UNLV's Special Collections.

The interior was spacious and offered air conditioning. The bar and casino had angled windows that looked out over the pool. Pink leather furnishings accented the soft greens in the wallpaper and carpet. A cantilevered roof over the walkway led out to the pool that had once been a gravel pit.

Across from the pool court, the hotel wing—dubbed the Oregon Building—was a three-story building of simple lines, which included a stepped-up fourth floor where Siegel's private suite was located. The suite was constructed with reinforced concrete and steel acquired from naval shipyards. Siegel's office was completely bullet-proof. An elevator with an anteroom outside the suite allowed for visitors to wait before entrance was allowed. Two stairway exits, one from the living room and one from the bedroom, led down to the other floors. A secret trap door in the bedroom included a ladder that led down to the basement, allowing swift passage should the need arise. A false stairway and hallways that led nowhere were installed to confuse those who had nefarious intentions.

The Flamingo opened on Dec. 26, 1946, featuring a showroom, lounge, and restaurant. In the showroom, Jimmy Durante, Xavier Cugat and his Orchestra, and Rose Marie were the headliners. Despite a winter storm that included rain, thunder, and lightning, some of Siegel's Los Angeles friends such as George Raft, Sonny Tufts, George Sanders, and Georgie Jessel braved the elements to board the plane that Siegel had chartered for the occasion. The hotel rooms weren't finished so guests had to find accommodations at other hotels. This proved to be a boon for the other hotels as the Flamingo guests would often take their winnings and continue gambling at the hotel where they were staying.

The bad weather forced many of the invited guests to send their regrets. The heralded grand opening that Siegel had so meticulously planned was being called a flop. To make matters worse, the casino lost over $300,000 the first two weeks to winning gamblers.

The Oregon Building with Ben Siegel's private suite overlooking the pool area at the Flamingo Hotel. Image courtesy of the Nevada State Museum, Las Vegas.

According to the *Hollywood Reporter* biography on founder Billy Wilkerson, Wilkerson took out an ad in the *Hollywood Reporter* and flaunted Siegel's cost overruns and irresponsible behavior.

Locals who attended the grand opening went home and told their friends about the opulent hotel where men were required to wear jacket and tie or, more preferably, a tuxedo, and women were required to wear evening gowns. For a small community like Las Vegas where the prevailing attitude was still "the early west in modern splendor" this was much too formal for many locals.

The high overhead costs, the few customers, and the mounting construction costs on the remaining, unfinished hotel rooms forced Siegel to temporarily close the resort. Cost overruns were rumored to be as high as $4 million. Siegel began borrowing money from anyone who would loan it to him. He hired a New York lawyer, Hank Greenspun, as his publicist.

Siegel planned on reopening the hotel in March 1947. The hotel rooms were completed without further interference and the second opening of the hotel was more of a success than the first. The Hollywood crowd came to see "Ben's" new resort and many of them liked what they saw.

Publicist Hank Greenspun was quoted as saying, "To capture its sweep and grandeur you have to be conditioned by a Goldwyn set that's been dolled up by Orson Welles. This Flamingo is indeed a most colorful and amazing bird." (*Las Vegas Life Magazine*, 1947)

Guests enjoy the lavish buffet at the Flamingo. Image courtesy of the Nevada State Museum, Las Vegas.

Revelers enjoy the music in the lounge at the Flamingo. Image courtesy of the J. Florian Mitchell Collection, Nevada State Museum, Las Vegas.

Part of the plumage: "105 beautifully appointed hotel rooms, a health club, gymnasiums, steam rooms, tennis, badminton, squash, and handball courts, stables with forty head of fine riding stock, a championship AAU specification swimming pool, a trapshooting range, nine hole golf course, nine different shops of national prominence ... "-Hank Greenspun, publisher *Las Vegas Life Magazine*, 1947.

The Flamingo included bingo as a way to lure the locals back. In less than two months, the hotel was showing a profit. However, for Siegel, it was not enough. His investors, tired of seeing an endless money pit, wanted a faster return on their dollars. A private meeting was called in Havana that was overseen by ex-patriate mobster, Charles "Lucky" Luciano.

When Siegel heard about the meeting, he flew to Havana and met personally with Luciano. Luciano demanded that Siegel start paying the investment back. Siegel, enraged, lost his famous temper and walked out.

Unbeknownst to Siegel, his mob investors and friends had had enough. A hit was ordered on the charismatic gangster who had come up the hard way with his pal, Meyer Lansky, on the mean streets of New York. Siegel was killed on June 20, 1947, while sitting on the sofa in the living room of Virginia Hill's Beverly Hills home. A shooter hid the rose bushes outside and then blasted nine bullets into Siegel, shooting out one of the famed gangster's blue eyes. Siegel's friend, Al Smiley, sitting across the room, was unharmed. Siegel's companion, Virginia Hill, had conveniently flown to Paris the previous day.

At the same time that Benjamin Siegel was finding out that money means more than blood to his mob friends, Moe Sedway, Gus Greenbaum, and Morris Rosen were walking into the Flamingo's casino and seizing control of the hotel. Peg Crockett's husband, George, the founder of local Alamo Airways and then owner of the airport, was there that evening.

[George and a friend were at the Flamingo and were] lucky enough to get one of the front row seats and they sat down to dinner and at this next table were expensively dressed men that George hadn't seen before. And George remarked to his friend how somber they were.

They just looked like morticians. The show came on and just before the show ended, one of the waiters came in and whispered to the man at the table next to George and word got around —all the way around the table and just before the show ended, they all got up and walked out. And George and Stu went into the casino and each one of those men were already there.

One of them walked to the casino cage and one of them walked to the front desk. One of them walked here and they all had their stations that they walked to and took over. And George said, "I wonder what's going on?" Well anyway, they went home and turned the radio on and found that Bugsy Siegel had been shot that night in California. And that was the take-over.

Peg Crockett interview with the author, 2005

When word of Siegel's murder hit the news wires, the town of Las Vegas figured prominently in the articles written about the mobster/hotel owner. It was the kind of advertising that the up-and-coming town needed, and it would reap the benefits for years to come.

Morris Rosen, after conferring with his partners, began putting the necessary money together to buy the property from Siegel's Nevada Projects Corporation company. In short order Rosen raised $3.9 million and bought the Flamingo. Hidden financial partners in the hotel were many well-known mob figures that included Meyer Lansky.

Renamed the Fabulous Flamingo, the gaming license was issued to Sanford Adler who served as manager and front man. Adler proved to be less of a shill than the silent partners were hoping for. A dispute soon flared over ownership with Adler filing a lawsuit. The case was heard by the Nevada Supreme Court which ruled in Adler's favor. After Adler got into a fist fight with Rosen, he realized what Billy Wilkerson had learned a few years earlier, that it was better to get out and live then stand on principle. Adler turned control of his shares over to local attorney Louis Weiner (who had also been Siegel's lawyer) and his partner, Cliff Jones, to sell.

Ladies line up to partake of the Flamingo's well-stocked buffet. Image courtesy of the J. Florian Mitchell Collection, Nevada State Museum, Las Vegas.

In 1948, Greenbaum took over the day-to-day running of the hotel. Within the year, the Fabulous Flamingo was showing a $4 million profit. Wilkerson and Siegel paved the way for others who wanted to build new sophisticated hotels and casinos in what was quickly becoming the hottest strip of land in the Southwest.

But in some ways, Siegel had the last laugh. A few years ago, television news-caster Diane Sawyer called him "the man who built Las Vegas" which must have come as a surprise to the people who had been living there since the early 1900s. Today, various books, magazines, and newspaper articles all link Siegel to the post-war future of Las Vegas.

THE FABULOUS FLAMINGO

The Las Vegas of the 1950s has become a mythic place. The Thunderbird, Wilbur Clark's Desert Inn, and The Sands Hotel all opened in the early 1950s, adding more glitz to the neon skyline of the Strip and more glamour to the experience. Hollywood had discovered Las Vegas and stars were performing in all the showrooms. Opening night in Las Vegas meant that not only would the performer's fans be in the audience but many of their Hollywood friends as well. It was not unusual to see stars such as Kirk Douglas, Yul Brynner, Elizabeth Taylor, Humphrey Bogart, and many others sitting front and center in King's Row of the various showrooms up and down the Strip.

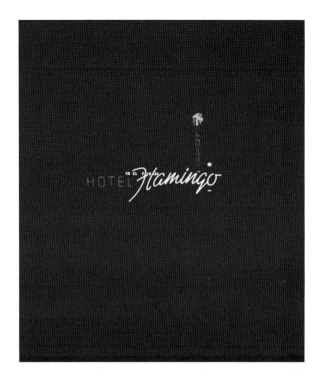

The original neon
signage at the
Flamingo Hotel.
Image courtesy of
the Nevada State
Museum, Las Vegas.

Under Gus Greenbaum's watchful eye, the Flamingo was turning a sizeable profit. Big band and jazz artists were featured in the lounge. Greenbaum hired Abe Schiller to handle publicity. Schiller, who dressed in pink, silk embroidered western shirts, along with other P.R. men, Al Freeman, Harvey Deiderich, Stan Irwin and Herb McDonald, became one of the most hard-working publicists on the Las Vegas Strip.

The opening of the Sands Hotel—a Place in the Sun—in 1952 compelled the Flamingo to spend $1 million in renovations and remodeling. The original entrance and signage was demolished and a new entrance with an upswept roof was built. A large, pink, neon sign that spelled out Flamingo in huge lettering was designed by Bill Clark of Ad-Art. A neon-bubbling Champagne Tower was added as well. The exterior neon for the tower was designed by the neon designers at YESCO.

In 1951, the Flamingo was one of the backdrops for *The Las Vegas Story*, a drama starring Victor Mature, Jane Russell, and Vincent Price. The film was directed by Robert Stevenson and produced by Howard Hughes, who owned R-K-O Studio at the time. It premiered in Las Vegas in February 1952, a few weeks after the official premiere in New York City.

Rendering of the new facade for the Flamingo Hotel. Image courtesy of UNLV's Special
Collections.

In 1955, Tommy Hull, who had built the El Rancho Vegas, put together a
group of mostly local and Hollywood investors and made an offer of $7 mil-
lion to buy the hotel. The Flamingo owners said yes. Other investors included
Chester Simms, George Raft, Jackie Gaughan, crooner Tony Martin, and Albert
Parvin, of Parvin-Dohrmann. Parvin was selected to be president of the hotel.
His company Parvin-Dohrmann had supplied the furnishings for many of the
young resorts on the Las Vegas Strip.

Everyone who was anyone (and not under contract to The Sands) performed
at the Fabulous Flamingo in the 1950s it seems. Among the marquee stars were
Louis Armstrong, Tony Martin, Mickey Rooney, Gracie Allen and George Burns,
the Three Stooges, Lena Horne, and the Spike Jones Band.

In 1955, a bandleader named Louis Prima, his singer-wife Keely Smith, and
saxophonist Sam Butera and his group, the Witnesses, took over the Casbar
Lounge at the Sahara. Their act revolutionized lounge entertainment in Las
Vegas. To stay up with the times, the Flamingo opened the revolving Stage Bar,
which featured name entertainment from dusk till dawn. The joint was, as they
used to say, jumping.

Even back then, the more high-end resorts like the Flamingo were being
described as self-contained cities. Three artesian wells on the property supplied
fresh water to the hotel and its customers, and there was a back-up power plant

ready to supply power to the hotel in case of a blackout. The resort also had its own heating plant and sewage system.

Also in 1955, Ed Levinson, an executive at the Flamingo, was tapped to become the president of the recently built Fremont Hotel. His partners gave him a going-away party and Chester Simms took over Levinson's duties at the Flamingo.

The Lou Basil Orchestra was brought in to replace the Teddy Phillips Orchestra. Lou Basil's daughter, Toni, would enroll and later become a cheerleader at Las Vegas High School before going on to record that hit pop song of the 1980s, "Hey, Mickey!"

The resort was averaging 2,000 guests a day, offered $4 full-course meals, and had 116 slot machines, 7 dice tables, 6 blackjack tables, and 3 roulette wheels.

In 1957, Abe Schiller, Stan Irwin of the Sahara, and Al Freeman of the Sands all participated in the Calgary Stampede. They were in the welcoming Canadian Parade throwing silver dollars to the crowd. The international promotion worked wonders for the hotels as pictures of the three, with Abe—in his pink, silk western shirt—throwing coins to the crowd, were sent to newspapers around the world.

In May 1958, Parvin again ordered the show stages remodeled and added another ninety-two rooms to the hotel. That brought the room total to 336 and the new rooms were ready to be occupied by Labor Day weekend.

As the 1950s came to a close, Abe Schiller was promoted to Executive Vice President of the Flamingo Hotel. The Las Vegas News Bureau, working with the hotel publicists, had done a remarkable job of marketing Las Vegas as a tourist destination.

The town that had once been marketed as "the early West in modern splendor" was now being marketed as the chic place to vacation. Guests were encouraged to gamble, drink, have a good time, and when they got home, tell their friends and neighbors all about it. Visiting Las Vegas became an option for more and more Americans.

In 1960, the Parvin-Dohrmann Company that owned the Flamingo decided it was time for a change. They put the hotel up for sale. It was bought by a syndicate of owners headed by Miami Beach hotelier Morris Lansburgh. Lansburgh reportedly was friends with Meyer Lansky. Lansky reportedly received a $200,000 finder's fee for putting the deal together.

During the sale, five men held on to their minority interests in the resort. The five men all had mid-western gaming roots. They were Edward J. Barrick and his partner Sam Ziegmann, John "Jackie" Gaughan, Morris Baker, and Chester Simms. Their total interest was said to be valued at $306,250. The Nevada Gaming Control Board allowed them to continue as licensees.

In April 1961, the Flamingo opened its new Convention Hall. The opening was a charity benefit for the March of Dimes. Steve Allen was the Master of Ceremonies and with his wife, actress Jayne Meadows, kept the evening lively.

Guests try their luck at the
Flamingo's craps table.
Image courtesy of UNLV's
Special Collections.

Lansburgh had pioneered the idea of "Cavalcade of Stars" in Miami—the idea was to utilize top name entertainment in his hotels in Miami and that had the effect of increasing room occupancy as well. While it was expensive, he thought the idea would work well in Las Vegas.

In May, the Musicians Union held a Jazz Festival at the resort. Some of the greatest names in jazz performed, including Lionel Hampton, Charlie Teagarden, and Vido Musso with Phil Harris as the Master of Ceremony. Six hundred jazz lovers enjoyed the swinging sounds.

The Flamingo was also gaining a reputation as the place to hear good jazz. Sarah Vaughan, Lionel Hampton, Della Reese, and Harry James were routinely playing the lounge.

KRAM-Radio had been a fixture on Las Vegas radio dials since the 1940s. A deal was signed where they would broadcast a late-night program called *Night People* six nights a week from the grounds of the Flamingo.

By 1962, Lansburgh was advertising that 600 hotel rooms at the Flamingo now had suites with motifs including French Provincial, Gay 90s, Japanese Modern, and the Old West. Most hotels would have gone with just one motif but not the Fabulous Flamingo.

The upgrade of rooms was quite successful and in October 1962, Lansburgh presided over the ground-breaking ceremonies for an additional 200 rooms.

An ad for the Driftwood Lounge featuring Ella Fitzgerald. Image courtesy of As We Knew It: Classic Las Vegas Collection.

Robert Goulet, fresh from his run on Broadway as Sir Lancelot in *Camelot*, made his Las Vegas debut at the Flamingo in January 1963.

That summer, the hotel was featured in a new Elvis Presley movie filming in town, *Viva Las Vegas*. The exterior shots of the hotel now provide a time capsule of sorts when viewing the film. *Viva Las Vegas* was filmed not only at the Flamingo, but the Convention Center Rotunda as well as downtown Fremont Street and UNLV's gym, which is now the Barrick Museum, named for the widow of the Flamingo's part-owner.

Fats Domino joined the line-up at the Driftwood Lounge. He was soon packing in crowds. Elvis Presley was spotted enjoying the show many times by locals.

Live albums recorded at Strip resorts were becoming best sellers. Bobby Darin recorded *The Curtain Falls-Live at the Flamingo*. Tom Jones had a best-selling album recorded at the Flamingo, *Tom Jones Live in Las Vegas*.

In the mid-1960s, the Flamingo came under investigation by the Nevada Gaming Control Board over the licensing of foreign investors. Ukio Kubota, president of the then Fujiya Nevada Corporation, applied for the purchase of

The Flamingo was the first hotel on the Strip to offer Japanese Houseboy Service. Image courtesy of UNLV's Special Collections.

the hotel through the issuing of $3 million worth of common stock. Kenjo Osano was the Japanese industrialist behind the money. The rule at that time was that a licensee had to be an American citizen. Rumors were rampant that Lansburgh and the majority stockholders were looking to sell the hotel because the Federal Government was investigating his New York gambling charters and rumors of skimming at the Flamingo as well as involvement by Meyer Lansky.

In 1967, the Sheraton Company announced they would lease the property once the sale was approved. However, in March of that year, the sale was canceled due to the failure of the new investors to get approval for licensing.

Kirk Kerkorian was part of the post-war Las Vegas tourist trade with his chartered high-stakes gaming flights as well as commercial aviation. In 1945, he bought a Cessna single engine plane for $5,000. He used the plane to train pilots and ferry high rollers to and from Las Vegas for high-stakes gaming. Two years later, he bought Trans International Air Service that consisted of three planes. In 1959, he changed the name to Trans International Airlines and became involved in passenger service on a whole new level. In 1962, he added a DC-8 jet and became the first to provide non-scheduled passenger jet service to Las Vegas. (K. J. Evans, *The First 100*)

Along the way, Kerkorian also made investments and bought land in Las Vegas as hotel-casinos were developing there in the 1950s and 1960s. His first investment was modest—$50,000 for a share of the Dunes Hotel in 1955. He lost his investment and resolved never again to invest in someone else's casino operation. In 1962, he bought 80 acres along the mid-Strip for $960,000. (K. J. Evans, *The First 100*)

Starting in the mid-1960s, Kerkorian rented his land on the mid-section of the Strip for $4 million to Jay Sarno for what would become Caesars Palace. He got part of that investment back in 1968 when he sold his Strip land to Sarno for $5 million. (K. J. Evans, *The First 100*)

In 1967, he surprised everyone by placing a bid for the Flamingo Hotel. His bid of $13 million for the hotel was quickly approved. In addition, he spent $5 million to acquire 65 acres on Paradise Road, about a half-mile east of the Strip, for what would become the International.

But, before he built the International, Kerkorian wanted to use the Flamingo as his training hotel to work out the problems of running a large resort hotel.

I joined Mr. Kerkorian in July, 1967. We decided to build what was known at that point as the International Hotel. We drew up plans and bought the property. And then I said, "Well, it's going to take approximately two years

Kirk Kekorian found great
success on the Las Vegas Strip.
Image courtesy of the Nevada
State Museum, Las Vegas.

to construct the hotel. And we really should have sort of a proving ground to put our team together for the International when it opens."

Fred Benninger to George Stamos in a 1979 interview. *Las Vegas Sun Sunday Magazine*, April 22, 1979

"I'm not a firm believer," Kerkorian told interviewer, Ken Evans, "that you have to have 30 years of experience, if you've got good, common sense. I can't take much credit except for seeing the big picture; the amount of rooms, what kind of showrooms, I'm into that part of it. But when you get the nitty-gritty, I don't have the education to really get in there and dissect it. I knew he could cut the mustard and he did. He helped, no, he built the International. He built the old MGM. It was all Fred Benninger.

K. J. Evans, *The First 100*

"All I knew about Las Vegas came from the other side of the table—the contributing end," Benninger recalled years later. (K. J. Evans, *The First 100*)

Kerkorian budgeted $2.5 million for renovations. Those renovations included the destruction of the famed neon champagne tower. There are still those in Las Vegas who miss that tower and its effervescent neon bubbles glowing skyward in the night.

Kerkorian added a 350-seat casino theater lounge with a new state of the art sound system that cost $50,000. He expanded the casino and hired architect, Martin Stern, Jr. Stern added a two-story *porte cochere*. A glass-enclosed restaurant, the Sky Room, was on the upper floor overlooking the Strip. The Flamingo became the first hotel that slowly advanced its property line to the sidewalk, pioneering the destruction of the Strip as an automobile driven by-way and heralding the forthcoming future of walking the Strip.

The Las Vegas Strip was filled with top of the line entertainment back then.

"You didn't come to Vegas to break in your act." entertainer Bob Anderson recounted in a 2004 interview with the author, "You came to Vegas to perform your act."

The marquees were filled with some of the greatest names in entertainment history. To get an idea of the cost of a show, consider this: The 1967 New Year's Eve dinner show at the Flamingo cost $30 per person. This was considered a high dollar amount back then. Wayne and Jerry Newton were the headliners with Jackie Kahane as the opening act. Dinner was served at 9:00 and the show started at 10:30. The $30 included dinner, the show, an attractive gift for each female guest, and a champagne breakfast in the hotel's McCarran Room. Today that same ticket would cost approximately $205, if not more after various fees and taxes.

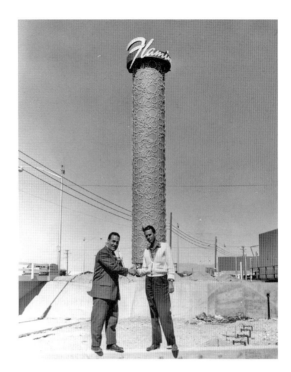

The Flamingo's famed
Champagne Tower was
demolished in a renovation
to update the hotel. Image
courtesy of UNLV's Special
Collections.

Kerkorian commissioned a twenty-eight-floor room tower and remodeled the famed Driftwood Lounge. It became the Flamingo Show Lounge and instead of focusing on jazz, Kerkorian signed pop groups like Kenny Rogers and the First Edition and the Spiral Staircase. The Flamingo Show Lounge was said to be the largest lounge in Las Vegas.

"The groups entertained back to back. Sometimes the place was so jammed you couldn't even get in the door," recalled long-time employee Dee Spencer. (*Las Vegas Sun Sunday Magazine*, April 22, 1979)

Kerkorian persuaded Alex Shoofey to leave the Sahara Hotel and appointed Shoofey resort president, a job he held until moving over to the International. Shoofey brought over Sahara entertainment director, Bill Miller, to work his magic at the Flamingo.

A new sign was commissioned for the front of the hotel.

The sign, designed by Bill Clarke of Ad-Art, was a combination of neon and incandescent light. Standing 130-feet tall, it was controlled by a state-of-the-art computer, the first one to do so. Its marquee panel was the largest freestanding panel of its kind and the sign was reported to cost $500,000. Placed almost to the sidewalk, at night, it filled the sky with pink and white neon.

The Flamingo Hotel in the late 1960s. Image courtesy of As We Knew It: Classic Las Vegas Collection.

Justice Department officials identified Meyer Lansky as a hidden partner in the former ownership. Skimming by the former regime was also suspected. Kerkorian's management of the Flamingo helped the feds make their case.

"The reason, I think, that they allowed us to go public," Kerkorian told Ken Evans, "was that I don't think the Flamingo ever showed anything more than $300,000 or $400,000 in profits. In our first year, 1968, we showed about $3 million." (K. J. Evans, *The First 100*)

In 1969, though they no longer owned the hotel, Lansburgh, Lansky, and several others were brought up on skimming charges—they were accused of skimming over $36,000,000 from the hotel between 1960 and 1967.

By 1970, Kerkorian had decided he was ready to open a new hotel. There was just one problem: money. He signed an agreement with Barron Hilton for both properties, the Flamingo and the International.

For Barron Hilton, though the Hiltons were famous for their hotels, this was his family's first venture into owning hotels, Las Vegas style. It was the first major corporate hotel chain to put its name on a hotel/casino in the state. A recent revision of Nevada gaming law now allowed that only officers of a corporation had to be licensed rather than each investor or member. This was instrumental for setting the stage for the changing face of the Las Vegas Strip. With new sources of corporate funds now available to be utilized, a new era of growth on the Strip was being born.

Rumors of the sale pegged the price at anywhere from $15 million to $37 million cash. Kerkorian remained the International's biggest stock holder, but he was already working on bigger and grander dreams of his next hotel. Kerkorian was said to have large debt obligations due to the loans he obtained in 1968 and 1969 to gain control of Western Airlines and MGM Studios. He received $5.5 million from the dividends of International Leisure stock, which he used to lower his debt.

In 1971, the hotel officially became the Flamingo Hilton. Later that year the Sky Room became the Speakeasy. Publicist Jim Seagrave remembers sending out invitations for the grand opening of the Speakeasy. Playing on former owner Siegel's "affiliations" the invitations invited VIPs to the opening courtesy of "Big Nick." (Interview with the author, 2005.)

Speaking of Siegel, his safe was discovered in the old Oregon Suite and it was decided that it should be opened and emptied.

Like Geraldo Rivera's stunt with Al Capone's safe, much was made in the media about the opening of Siegel's safe. And like Capone's safe, there was nothing to report when it was finally opened.

Writer Hunter S. Thompson and his attorney, Oscar Zeta Acosta, stayed at the Flamingo while attending a seminar for the National Conference of District Attorneys on Narcotics and Dangerous Drugs at the nearby Dunes Hotel. They had been staying at the Mint on Fremont Street while covering the famed Mint 400 race. Both events became mythic in Thompson's acclaimed *Fear and Loathing in Las Vegas: A Savage Journey to the Heart of the American Dream.*

In 1973, local judge Roger Foley ruled that Meyer Lansky be tried separately on skimming charges. Lansburgh had pled guilty on two counts of skimming. The other defendants in the case had all opted to stand trial. Lanksy was the only defendant who failed to appear in court. Foley ordered him to stand trial separately.

In the summer of 1975, a major thunderstorm hit the Las Vegas Valley. In a short amount of time, a record rainfall turned into a flash flood warning. At that time, Caesars Palace sat in the old Flamingo Wash. There were no storm drain provisions or safety measures. The southwest area was primarily desert without much development between the mountains and the Strip. The torrent of water came rushing down the Flamingo Wash. It roared through the parking lot at Caesars. Public announcements were made for guests to move their cars

A flash flood roared across the Las Vegas Strip on July 3, 1975. Image courtesy of As We Knew It: Classic Las Vegas Collection.

immediately. Most of the announcements went unheeded. The wall of water continued through Caesars parking lot, pushing cars into the low pony wall or overturning them all together. The water jumped the curb and continued across Las Vegas Blvd. where it rushed into the casino of the Flamingo Hotel. Patrons were seen standing in ankle deep water continuing to gamble.

That year the Hilton Corporation remodeled the Flamingo. They added a new tower, and built a new *porte cochere*, this one pushing right out to the sidewalk.

They also added a new neon sign designed by young sign designer, Raul Rodriquez. It was a three-dimensional flower of pink neon waving in the breeze. It made the statement that the Flamingo was leaving its roots behind and moving towards the future. The sign, manufactured by Heath and Company, was a break from the simpler marquee signs of the day.

By the end of the 1970s, the Flamingo Hilton boasted 2,250 rooms. It still had its lush gardens and its swanky swimming pool now boasted a towering water fountain and a twelve-seat Jacuzzi. The last remnants of the Siegel era, the Oregon Building, still rimmed the back of the pool area.

With a proposed $130-million-dollar renovation in 1993 and the need to stay competitive in the new Vegas Strip, the Hilton Corporation tore down the

The Raul Rodriquez designed sign was a break with tradition. Image courtesy of As We Knew It: Classic Las Vegas Collection.

Oregon Building including Siegel's private suite and the remaining 489 "Garden Rooms"—the old-fashioned motel-style rooms that had been a fixture of the original hotel.

A Wildlife Habitat was added that included African penguins (which have since been moved to the Dallas Zoo), Chilean flamingos, koi, ducks, swans, and goldfish as part of the renovation. The habitat's 15 acres of Caribbean-themed foliage and exotic wildlife is open to the public.

A year later, the Hilton Corporation constructed two 612-room towers costing $104 million. The tower contained 201 timeshare suites. The Hilton Grand Vacations became the first timeshare built on a major resort property.

In December 1998, the Hilton Hotels Corporation split lodging and gaming operations into separate divisions. This tax-free distribution to stockholders resulted in Park Place Entertainment Corporation being formed. In the split, the Flamingo, Bally's, and the Las Vegas Hilton became the property of Park Place. Shareholders were given one share of Park Place for each share of Hilton stock they owned. The deal included a two-year license to use the Hilton name.

When the license expired in 2000, Park Place chose not to renew it and the name of the hotel changed to Flamingo Las Vegas.

The Flamingo rang in the twenty-first century on December 31, 1999, with a party that started at 8:00 p.m. Robert Goulet provided the entertainment, and dinner, champagne, and party favors were included in the $225 a person ticket.

A plaque was installed in the gardens surrounding the pool area memorializing Benjamin Siegel and his accomplishments.

There is no plaque for Billy Wilkerson.

Today, the Flamingo Las Vegas continues to hold its own amid more construction, more mega-resorts and the changing face of the Las Vegas Strip.

Hopefully, wherever he is, Billy Wilkerson is smiling.

A room service menu from the Flamingo Hotel. Image courtesy of UNLV's Special Collections.

5

THE THUNDERBIRD
1948-2000

A DREAM IS BORN

When I was younger, I was fascinated by the Thunderbird signage. A big, beautiful neon encrusted mythic Thunderbird, that at one time I'm told, also bellowed smoke. Unfortunately, the upkeep and the need for natural gas to produce the smoke soon brought the majestic bird's days of smoking to an end. Still, at night it was one of the most beautiful signs ever created for the Classic Las Vegas Strip.

The Thunderbird Hotel began life as a dream shared by two good friends, local attorney Cliff Jones and general contractor, Marion Hicks. Hicks had run a gambling cruise ship and had built the El Cortez on Fremont Street in downtown Las Vegas.

However, Marion Hicks liked to dream big. In 1946, Jones and Hicks had bid on a hotel in Reno but that didn't work out as planned because they were outbid. Returning to Las Vegas still dreaming large, they discussed their possibilities. They both agreed that building a hotel on Highway 91 (today Las Vegas Blvd. South) would be the best idea. There were already two hotels on that stretch of the highway, the El Rancho Vegas and the Hotel Last Frontier, that were doing good business. The Flamingo was under construction but beset with building delays due to shortages created by World War II. Though the war had recently ended, the shortage of construction material was still a problem.

Deciding to wait until building supplies were more easily attainable, they set out to find the right piece of property. Guy McAfee, former owner of the land where the Hotel Last Frontier now stood and currently the owner of the Golden Nugget on Fremont Street, owned the land they wanted. The three men negotiated a deal—and wouldn't you have wanted to be a fly on the wall listening to that! The property fronted on 1,100 feet of the Highway. Hicks, Jones, and McAfee also bought a piece of land behind the Highway along Paradise Road.

The Thunderbird Hotel, the fourth hotel on the Las Vegas Strip. Image courtesy of the Nevada State Museum, Las Vegas.

In October 1947, building code restrictions were finally loosened and a small groundbreaking ceremony took place on the Strip-fronted property. Hicks had the reputation for building sturdy structures. The Thunderbird, like the El Cortez (which Hicks had also built), utilized "weeping mortar" which created a uniquely Southwestern look for the building. The two partners decided on the name Thunderbird, which was based on a Navajo legend.

The interiors, also designed by Hicks, carried this theme throughout the hotel. Warm, earthen colors were used, and the walls were decorated with Indian portraits. The cocktail lounge displayed murals of cowboys, chuck wagons, and saguaro cactus. The Wigwam Room and the Navajo Room also contributed to the Southwestern flair.

While Benjamin Siegel was going broke making the Flamingo the first carpet joint in town, Jones and Hicks went in another direction. They chose to make the Thunderbird's interior intimate and home-like. Three major fireplaces in the main public area added to the feeling of coziness.

On Labor Day, 1948, the hotel opened. Jake Katleman of the El Rancho Vegas and Farmer Page of the Pioneer Club were among the invited guests. During the

The front facade of the Thunderbird Hotel. Image courtesy of the Cliff Segerblom Collection, Nevada State Museum, Las Vegas.

grand opening, following in the footsteps of the other hotels, Jones and Hicks had "complimentary play." According to publicist Jack Melvin this was a gesture of goodwill by established hotel owners as well as an attempt to stimulate opening night action at the tables by encouraging gamblers to bet more.

However, Jones and Hicks soon found themselves in a rather precarious situation. Katleman, Page, and several other well-known owners won so much at the tables that evening that they literally won the hotel away from Jones and Hicks. Luckily for the two owners, a compromise was negotiated that allowed them to keep the hotel.

The Thunderbird immediately made a splash. It had the first *porte cochere,* a covered-roof entrance leading to the entrance lobby and casino. Also helping, nearby McCarran Airport opened that same year.

The Airport had an adobe-style front as well. The broad sloping roof of the Thunderbird had the simple gable of an overgrown bunkhouse but the lines supporting that *porte cochere* were crisp and modern.

In a throwback to its western roots, a small white rail fence edged the leading southern section of the property.

The Thunderbird with its majestic neon birds and the nearby Mobil station Pegasus helped make the classic Las Vegas Strip a neon paradise. Image courtesy of UNLV's Special Collections.

The room wings mimicked the Flamingo's style with a central three-story section raised above the two-story wings. In front of it was the pool with a high dive, palm trees, and lawn. The desert seemed to surround it all.

And it had that beautiful neon Thunderbird. The giant neon bird sat atop the observation tower with its giant talons seeming to grip the top of the tower. The neon bird was all the colors of the rainbow and made a fitting mate for the nearby neon Flamingo gracing the front of its neighboring casino.

The main Thunderbird was flanked by two smaller birds and was created by Graham Neon Sign Company. With a nearby Mobil station and its neon Pegasus and the neon windmill atop the El Rancho Vegas, the Las Vegas Strip seemed to be ready-made for the automobile traveler.

The hotel was also very successful. Part of that success was due to the loyal and courteous staff that Jones and Hicks had hired. Former boxer, "Gentleman" Gene Delmont was the casino host and Hicks recruited some of his best chefs from the El Cortez. With the success of the El Cortez, Marion Hicks was an established gaming veteran with a reputation for excellence, and he brought that same dedication to his new hotel.

Not wanting to get over-extended too quickly (which was to plague many owners after them), Jones and Hicks assembled a weathered team of investors and partners that helped ensure smooth and prosperous times for everyone. Joe Wells, the owner of Wells Cargo and the namesake of the very popular (and fondly remembered) Joe's Oyster Bar; Victor Sayer, owner of the Commercial Electric Company; Jack Lane, president of American Pipe and Steel; and Paul Wagoner, a land and mining expert, were all in the top echelon of investors and partners. Locals were tapped as well and included Guy McAfee, Jake Kozloff, Harry Badger, Bill Deer, "Tutor" Scherer, and "Buck" Blaine. They all added their knowledge of Nevada gaming to the pot.

Between 1952 and 1953, to accommodate overflow crowds staying at the hotel, the owners built a 110-room motel next door to their property and called it the Algiers. Guests at the Algiers were afforded the same perks and benefits as those staying at the Thunderbird. Next, the Terrace Room was added in December,1954 and was open for breakfast, lunch, and dinner. Situated next to the main dining room, it was designed to seat 450 guests. A second-floor banquet room was added a short time later.

All the expertise of the various investors did not, however, keep the Thunderbird from having its license suspended in 1955. The Nevada Tax Commission was the authority for state gaming. The Commission alleged that Jones and Hicks had not reported substantial investments by three underworld figures: Jake and Meyer Lansky and George Saldo. An injunction allowed the hotel to continue operating while the case went through the court system. After prolonged litigation, the Nevada Supreme Court ruled in favor of the Thunderbird, clearing the owners of all charges and revoking the suspension order. The court also upheld the state's ability and right to regulate casinos.

Entertainment-wise, Jones and Hicks, like the other resort owners, wanted top-of-the-line performers. Luckily, in that era, there were plenty of top notch acts to fill the bill. Hicks hired show producer Hal Braudis away from the Hotel Last Frontier to become the entertainment, publicity, and advertising director at the Thunderbird. Braudis brought with him his assistant, Barney Rawlings.

"Hal Braudis was a brilliant innovator and entertainment pioneer," remembered Rawlings in a 1979 interview. "He produced 'Miniature Musicals' which were cameos of current Broadway shows. He also did salutes to other Las Vegas hotels as well as introducing scenery sets to the otherwise rectangular dance floor. He also introduced a phrase that was to become a trademark of the hotel for many years: 'Remember, you saw it first at the Thunderbird.'"
Las Vegas Sun Sunday Magazine, May 6, 1979

Braudis hired Rosemary Clooney and as her opening act, Harry Belafonte. He hired the Mills Brothers, Patti Page, Burl Ives, and George Gobel. Opera stars such as James Melton and Dorothy Warrensjold also graced the showroom stage. The Dinner Show cost four dollars back then. The Late Show had a two-drink minimum with drinks under a dollar.

Rex Allen and the Sons of the Pioneers made showroom history one night. Allen performed with his horse "Coco." On this particular night, Coco violated the rule of all animal acts—all over the stage.

Barney Rawlings recalled in an interview with George Stamos:

> … the stage was table-top height and the incident occurred during the dinner show. The Lighting Director, Bob Ogle, quickly killed the stage lights and threw a spot on Rawlings. While pianist Fritz Becker began to play, stage hands frantically tried to clean the mess up. Becker went into the arpeggio for *Tenderly*, a popular love song of the day. So with the air conditioning circulating the barnyard aroma, I sang "the evening breeze caressed the trees tenderly" which brought the house down. After the laughter subsided, we got on with the show and I said "Remember, folks, you saw it first at the Thunderbird!" The audience roared with laughter.
>
> *Las Vegas Sun Sunday Magazine*, May 6, 1979

Fritz Becker remained at the Thunderbird for the next fourteen years. The Thunderbird also hosted the Branding Iron dinners. This dinner was held annually by the Las Vegas Press Club and offered a riotous evening of lampooning everyone from the governor to local officials.

"Everyone took an interest in those shows. They were sold out for months. My job was to write the arrangements so that we could all stop and start at the same time," Becker explained. (*Las Vegas Sun Sunday Magazine*, May 6, 1979)

Rose Marie, who often played the Thunderbird, remembered lounging in the pool at the Thunderbird and marveling at all the empty desert for as far as the eye could see. She brought a hand-held movie camera with her and shot home movies around the pool and grounds of the hotel.

In 1955, the owners expanded the casino, moving it out toward the street. They built a second floor that was framed with a rectangular box. A new *porte cochere* was added as well as a taller sign pole with three pennant signboards attached. The neon thunderbird was gently lifted into the air and came to rest on a pylon that now sat on top of the new *porte cochere*. The resort closed the Navajo Room for six weeks for remodeling. Work was carried out around the clock to ensure the re-opening before the annual New Year's Eve celebration. In the early 1960s, Joe Wells built a racetrack behind the hotel, aptly called Thunderbird Downs. The five-eighths of a mile race track hosted both thoroughbreds and quarter horses. It had pari-mutuel betting and temporary bleachers.

And they're at the gate at Thunderbird Downs! Image courtesy of Carey Burke.

The Lounge at the Thunderbird was the Pow-Wow Room and boasted a small stage, bar, and fireplace, making for an intimate place to enjoy some great music. Senator Pat McCarran became a regular at the hotel and Hicks had a four-room bungalow built for him. Howard Hughes was often spotted in the showroom, usually arriving after the show had started. Wilbur and Toni Clark spent many evenings there while the Desert Inn was under construction.

The Thunderbird had the first convention sales manager and hosted what was likely the first convention on the Strip, a gathering of air-conditioning specialists, much of whose time was spent cavorting on Lake Mead. Chef Jack Collins improvised a barbecue for them, according to legend, by welding two automobile axles together and roasting a steer.

Nat King Cole began performing there in 1948.

Unlike other hotels, where the performers had to go through the kitchen to reach the stage, the Thunderbird was designed so that the performers didn't have to take such a circuitous route. Abe Fox, the owner of Foxy's Deli, remembered delivering meals to Cole at a trailer the performer had next to the hotel. This was during the time of segregation and Cole could not stay in the hotel. Rather than commute each night after his shows, to the Westside, Cole stayed in the trailer. When Jack Entratter stole Cole away to perform at the Sands, the trailer went with him.

The Thunderbird also had the first semi-nude Ice Show on the Strip. George Arnold, a well-known skater, was tapped to produce the show.

Nat King Cole onstage. Image courtesy of UNLV's Special Collections.

When I was asked to come out here from New York and produce the Ice Show, I had never seen a nude ice show before. I actually had to ask my father and mother for permission to produce the show, *Ecstasy on Ice*. The show ran for over three years. It even made the cover of *Time* magazine.

Las Vegas Sun Sunday Magazine, May 6, 1979

GLORY DAYS

Marion Hicks died in 1961. He had retired to Palm Springs, leaving his nephew Marty, Cliff Jones, and Joe Wells to run the hotel.

In 1963, producer Monte Proser announced that he had exclusive rights from Rodgers and Hammerstein to produce their musicals in Las Vegas. He opened with *Flower Drum Song* starring Jack Soo. This was the first time an abridged version of the musical had been produced. It was deemed a success and *South Pacific* with Mitzi Gaynor soon followed. In 1964, the owners sold the hotel to Del Webb for approximately $9.5 million, and Webb leased the hotel to a corporation headed by Herbert Lodge. Lodge was a Miami businessman and former owner of the Golden Nugget in Miami Beach. The new management brought in Jerry Schafer who pioneered afternoon entertainment.

The Thunderbird Hotel with the Mobil Pegasus in the background. Image courtesy of As We Knew It: Classic Las Vegas Collection.

Souvenir cover from the Thunderbird Hotel. Image courtesy of As We Knew It: Classic Las Vegas Collection.

In 1965, the Thunderbird was remodeled, and the new front facade included the longest sign constructed at that time. It was a free-standing billboard that had letters that stood out on a bed of gold light, echoing the Shell sign across the street. According to neon sign designer Betty Willis, the new Thunderbird sign was the first in the modernization of neon that began in the mid-1960s.

It was designed by Ad-Art and the massive, pulsating display was the longest, continuous length sign in the world. It measured over 700 feet long and included 37,000 sparkling light bulbs. Eight miles of neon tubing and over 140,000 feet of wiring were used in the construction. Special power lines had to be brought in to accommodate the drain on electrical lines. The free-standing pylon was kept as well as the original Thunderbird. Bill Clarke designed the signage, which cost nearly $250,000 and took about 10,000 man hours to construct.

At night, the sparkling facade proclaimed the Thunderbird's title by sequentially flashing the neon letters and then silhouetting the letters with the thousands of bulbs that formed the backdrop.

However, even with that beautiful sign, the monthly lease of $19,000 kept the hotel from keeping pace with the rapidly changing and growing Strip. Webb finally foreclosed on the group in December 1967.

In 1972, the Thunderbird changed hands again. Though hopes were high on Halloween night, representatives from Caesars World, which owned both Caesars and the Thunderbird, came into the casino and confiscated all the

The new Thunderbird facade and sign. Image courtesy of As We Knew It: Classic Las Vegas Collection.

chips. Caesars' executives revealed plans for the Thunderbird to be demolished to make room for a twin towered hotel called the Marc Antony.

Perhaps luckily, the Marc Antony was never built. Soon after realizing that the Thunderbird was a drain on their bottom line, Caesars World sold the hotel to a group of local investors headed by Bank of Las Vegas legend, Parry Thomas. Thomas and his group bought it for $9 million, four million less than what Caesars World had paid for it.

Thomas and his group ran the hotel, now very down on its luck, until January 1, 1977, when Major Riddle, then-owner of the Dunes, bought the hotel. Riddle had the reputation, somewhat deservedly, of being a miracle worker with older properties.

Riddle opted to close the Thunderbird and rename the hotel the Silverbird.

On August 8, 1978 —just shy of its thirtieth anniversary—the giant neon Thunderbird was removed from the Las Vegas Strip forever. The front facade was changed but the buildings in the back remained. They renamed the lounge The Silver Star. The Showroom was rechristened the Continental Theater and featured Redd Foxx and *Playgirls on Ice '77*.

By 1980, the Silverbird had over 400 rooms and suites. Restaurants included the Terrace Room Coffee Shop, La Paloma, and the gourmet room, Top Brass. The casino now boasted 80,000 square feet and offered baccarat, a race and sports book, a poker room, Keno lounge, and a bingo parlor.

Following in the footsteps of others, Major Riddle offered the "Silverspree," which for $59.95 offered a visitor three days and two nights at the hotel. This spree also included a late show in the Continental Theater, two cocktails during that show, a free drink for enjoying the show in the casino lounge, a free drink for enjoying the show in the New Silver Star Lounge, one buffet dinner, one free Keno ticket and baggage handling upon arrival and departure (which was free to begin with).

In late 1981, Ed Torres, a veteran operator, bought the Silverbird and added Spanish-style mission architecture to the front. He renamed the hotel the El Rancho, thus creating confusion for years to come for people talking about the El Rancho Vegas. This El Rancho opened in 1982 and the buildings had been renamed to reflect a Western past: Dodge City, Virginia City, and Carson City. A tower was built, and a fifty-two-lane bowling center was installed. When the casino was expanded to 90,000 square feet, a new Race and Sports Book was added. Joe's Oyster Bar, though Joe Wells was long gone by now, was rechristened Joe's Stone Crab Restaurant. In 1982, Rodney Dangerfield opened his own comedy club inside the El Rancho, Rodney's Place.

In 1987, Torres made history by appointing the first female casino manager, Danou Sears. Sears arrived from France in 1963 and had been a dancer with the *Casino de Paris* show at the Dunes. She was with the troupe for eight years before leaving to join Barry Ashton and his new show at the Union Plaza.

She left dancing in 1972 and became a blackjack dealer at the Horseshoe Club. Torres had hired her to work at the Riviera and then the Aladdin. While at the Aladdin she had become a shift boss. There were few women in the pit, much less upper echelons of the casino in those days.

The El Rancho tried to hold on, but the Las Vegas Strip was undergoing the beginnings of a massive transformation, which would alter the face of the boulevard forever and change the way people visit Las Vegas. On June 30, 1992, the El Rancho closed the Sports Book, a cocktail lounge and the bingo parlor, and the slot machines were unplugged. One day later, the bowling alley and coffee shop closed. On July 6, 1992, the hotel and casino were closed.

In November 1993, Las Vegas Entertainment Network, a Los Angeles based television production company, purchased the property for $36.5 million. The new owners promised to transform the ailing property into Countryland USA, a country and Western themed hotel. They revealed plans for two hotel towers shaped like cowboy boots, a rodeo arena and a country-themed amusement park. Hoping to cash in on the idea of Las Vegas as family destination, they had big dreams.

That's all they were though, just dreams. The company defaulted on the $12 million note in November 1994. Though given an extension until the following August, the company agreed to pay 18% interest on the loan, but it's anyone's guess why such a deal was considered a good idea in the first place. LVEN publicly stated that it needed $300,000 a month to meet cash expenditures and it was at risk for losing its one asset, the El Rancho (nee Thunderbird).

Despite intervention by John Bryan and Whatley Investments, the company again defaulted on the payment in August 1995. They were given until December 1 to make the payment or lose the property. In February 1996, Orion Casino Corporation, a newly formed Nevada subsidiary of International Thoroughbred Breeders, purchased the 21-acre El Rancho property from LVEN for $43.5 million.

It may be hard to believe, but the Orion Corporation had even bigger stars in their eyes than LVEN. They quickly announced plans to add a $1 billion multi-casino project called the Starship Orion. Company officials bragged of 5.4 million square feet of hotel, casino, and retail/entertainment space all done in a modern space age theme. They announced it would open in August 1998.

By now, you may be wondering if there was something in the water all these folks were drinking, for it certainly seems like they were looking at this piece of property on the Las Vegas Strip and losing all common sense. Alas, they cannot blame it on their water. I guess they will have to blame it on the stars.

As plans went ahead, there was talk of seven separately owned and operated casinos, an alien circus, theaters, and various interactive and motion-based entertainment rides. The centerpiece was to be a constellation-class space ship that would be 750 feet in circumference. Interior passageways would connect

1,000 first-class passenger cabins to the dining areas and Sports Book, presumably, because even in space, you still want to gamble.

The Star Trek-type dream soon fell apart. New Jersey Horse Racing Association bought the property but before they could get too many stars in their eyes and reveal plans for another unworkable hotel, Clark County deemed the property an eyesore. Destruction of the buildings on the property began in June 1999, but was soon halted over a controversy about demolition permits.

In May 2000, a Florida-based company, Turnberry Associates, stepped in and bought the property for $45 million. Turnberry was building two condominium towers on Paradise Road and was advertising to the elite of Las Vegas to move in. Promising spectacular views of the Las Vegas Strip, Downtown, and the mountains, the view did not include the crumbling facade of the El Rancho (*née* Thunderbird). The garden room motel suites, the last remaining vestiges of the Thunderbird, were the first to go.

On October 3, 2000, the Thunderbird/Silverbird/El Rancho was imploded. It only took 700 pounds of explosives to bring her down.

"When the Thunderbird opened," Bud Weill, a local disc jockey remembered, "it was unquestionably the most magnificent structure in Las Vegas ... it lent something to the city. It was just a fun, fun place to be." (*Las Vegas Sun Sunday Magazine*, May 6, 1979)

A bathing beauty enjoys the pool area at the Thunderbird Hotel. Image courtesy of the J. Florian Mitchell Collection, Nevada State Museum, Las Vegas.

6

WILLIAM CLARK'S DESERT INN
1950-2000

A DREAM COMES TRUE

> Wilbur Clark gave me my first job in Las Vegas. That was 1951. For six bucks
> you got a filet mignon dinner and me.
>
> Frank Sinatra, 1992

The first hotels on the Las Vegas Strip were known by their names, El Rancho
Vegas, the Hotel Last Frontier, the Fabulous Flamingo, and the Thunderbird. A
visionary with an early sense of branding decided that his new hotel would be
different and so, Wilbur Clark's Desert Inn was born. The hotel would become
world famous, even long after Clark himself had shuffled off this mortal coil.

Wilbur Clark came to Las Vegas in a roundabout way. He grew up in Keyesport,
Illinois, but longed to go west. At nineteen, he decided to hitchhike to San Diego
in search of new adventures. When he finally got there, he found work at the
Knickerbocker Hotel as a bellman.

Clark was a shrewd businessman with big dreams. Always a resourceful fellow,
he soon owned thirteen bars in the San Diego area. In 1938, he traveled to Las
Vegas for the first time. He was underwhelmed with the business opportunities
that the small dusty railroad town had to offer.

Six years later, however, Las Vegas was in the midst of a boom cycle thanks
to World War II. When Clark returned in 1944, the town offered more to those
who dreamed big. He immediately recognized the possibilities that Highway
91 had to offer those tourists arriving by car from California. Tommy Hull was
looking to move on from the El Rancho Vegas, and Clark bought in, becoming
a majority owner. He also invested in the Players Club.

While visiting downtown Las Vegas, Clark realized that Fremont Street was
also moving away from its community roots and was reshaping itself to be a
tourist destination. The Northern Club on the south side of Fremont Street

Wilbur Clark's Desert Inn became a great example of early branding. Image courtesy of the Nevada State Museum, Las Vegas.

caught his eye. In 1931, when gambling was legalized in the state, owner Mayme Stocker had received the first gaming license from the city of Las Vegas.

The Club had done land-office business back then—thanks, in part, to being near the train depot which provided a steady stream of thirsty customers who were just passing through. By the time Clark was showing interest, Stocker was looking to retire, so Clark leased the space and then re-named it the Monte Carlo Club.

But Clark dreamt of designing and owning a major resort on the Las Vegas Strip that would cater to high rollers and provide the best in entertainment. He knew that once the war was over, Americans would want to travel again after years of rationing and supporting the war effort. He looked at this oasis in the desert and saw a future that he could help build and shape through his own vision.

His dream resort would become the Desert Inn, named after a hotel that he liked in Palm Springs. In 1945, he bought the land across the highway from the Last Frontier and, a year later, he sold his interest in the El Rancho Vegas for $1.5 million.

By 1946, the Strip was already showing growing pains. Billy Wilkerson and his partner, Benjamin Siegel, were building—and fighting over—the Fabulous Flamingo, and Cliff Jones and Marion Hicks were in the planning stages of the Thunderbird.

In 1947, construction began on Wilbur Clark's Desert Inn. However, Clark was soon short of funds due to the high costs of building materials and construction costs in the post-war era.

Mayme Stocker, owner of the
Northern Club, leased the club to
Wilbur Clark, who renamed it the
Monte Carlo Club. Image courtesy
of UNLV's Special Collections.

Wilkerson and Siegel had the same problem, but Siegel was able to talk his east coast friends such as Meyer Lansky and others into footing the bill. Hicks and Jones had decided to delay construction on their hotel until the cost of building materials stabilized.

Clark was forced to stop construction and the partially built resort sat vacant and incomplete. Locals would ride their horses out to the property to see if Clark had gotten lucky and started back up. As the months dragged on, Clark's folly in the desert became the butt of jokes told around town.

In December 1946, Siegel—having muscled out partner Billy Wilkerson—opened the Flamingo and laid claim to opening the first modern hotel in post-war Las Vegas.

Clark realized that his dream would not become a reality without some help. He approached Moe Dalitz and a group of investors that included Morris Kleinman, Sam Tucker, and Tom McGinty. They were all from Cleveland, part of the Mayfield Road Gang, and every one of them had bootlegging and gambling experience. Clark sold them 75% of his interest in return for the funds to finish the hotel.

Construction finally started back up again in 1949. Designed by Wayne McAllister and Hugh Taylor, the weeping mortar and native stone were, according

Hermon Boernge's sketch of the Desert Inn signage. Image courtesy of the Boernge Family.

to Alan Hess, "composed in a clean-lined modern design, half ranch house, half nightclub." (Alan Hess, *Viva Las Vegas: After-Hours Architecture*)

The fanciful neon sign was designed by YESCO's Hermon Boernge and featured a saguaro cactus, a species not found in Southern Nevada, but grown in Arizona. "But it was a pretty cactus," recalled architect Hugh Taylor.

Jac Lessman, who Dalitz had recommended, designed the interiors. As both Clark and Dalitz wanted more glamour than Old West charm, Hugh Taylor replaced McAllister.

Taylor and Clark traveled around the country to different resorts to get ideas. Clark was particularly fond of the Desert Inn Hotel in Palm Springs with is Spanish-style bungalows, and thick adobe walls. Dalitz insisted that Clark and Taylor visit the Beverly Hills Club near Cincinnati to see how a real casino operated. The Club catered to a well-heeled crowd and offered a spacious dining room, a lavish showroom, and a casino. In Cincinnati, the casino had to be well-hidden as gambling was illegal. In Las Vegas, though, the casino could be front and center.

Hugh Taylor, constantly taking notes, took the ideas that Clark and Dalitz wanted most and incorporated them into the design features of the Desert Inn. In doing so, he raised the bar even higher than Siegel had with the Fabulous Flamingo.

Clark continued to travel, always on the lookout for new ideas.

According to Alan Hess, after a trip to San Francisco's Mark Hopkins Hotel with its Top of the Mark lounge, Clark returned wanting a similar lounge for the Desert Inn. Thus, the Sky Room was born. The three-story tower dominated the facade of the new hotel and was, for a while, the tallest building on the Strip.

> Glass enclosed on three sides, this lounge is reminiscent of an airport lookout tower. The surrounding desert, mountains and far-reaching tropically landscaped grounds are clearly visible at all times. At night, tiny electric stars twinkling in the ceiling of the lounge make it seem one with the surrounding desert.
>
> Reviewer for *Architect and Engineer*

The twinkling sky at night gave patrons the feeling of floating in the sky. "Meet me at the Sky Room" became a popular saying around town. The Sky Room overlooked the "Dancing Waters," a series of rising and falling fountains in the figure-8 shaped pool that were set to pre-recorded music and lit by colored lights. (Alan Hess, *Viva Las Vegas: After-Hours Architecture*)

Clark may not have owned a controlling interest in the hotel any longer, but he was determined to have his name attached to the hotel.

Many a Las Vegas couple spent a lovely evening on the town at the Sky Room. Image courtesy of Carey Burke.

He and his wife, Toni, along with a small group of friends, had lived in a small nearby motel while Clark had searched for the financing to complete his dream. They would visit the site regularly and give Clark pep talks that kept him going. They celebrated holidays, birthdays, and anniversaries in that small hotel, never letting Clark give up on his dream.

Thanks in no small part to that encouragement, Clark's dream became a reality. At the street entrance was an old-fashioned ranch sign that said Wilbur Clark's Desert Inn in script across the top. A circular drive led up to the entrance which was a broad porch lined with ashlar pillars and lounge chairs. In the middle of the lawn was a fountain that sprayed water sixty feet into the air.

The stone was Bermuda pink with green trim. The hotel wings were interspersed around the pool patio with the parking lots behind the main building, and the majority of the clientele arrived by automobile and appreciated the ample free parking. The cinder block structure had a sandstone veneer quarried in Arizona and Nevada. Redwood was used throughout the interior and the flooring was flagstone. The entire resort was air-conditioned with the innovation of individual thermostats in each room.

Clark had hired Hank Greenspun as his publicity director. Greenspun sent invitations to all the major newspapers and magazines. The budget for transportation and lodging of the media guests was over $5,000.

Beauties hanging out next to the entrance of Wilbur Clark's Desert Inn. Image courtesy of Carey Burke.

Clark himself sent out 150 invitations to VIPs he knew personally and gave each of them a $10,000 credit limit. Dalitz and his crew also sent out personal invitations to the grand opening. (*Las Vegas Sun Magazine*, May 29, 1979)

A chef from the renowned Ritz Hotel in Paris, Maurice Thominet, oversaw the Gourmet Room. Allard Roen, who worked for Dalitz, managed the casino.

Wilbur Clark's Desert Inn had two openings in April 1950. The first one, held on April 24, was for those special by-invitation-only VIPs and the second one the next day was for the general public. It had cost $4.5 million to build the resort and it sported 229 rooms. *New Yorker* writer A. J. Liebling called it a "moderately gigantic temple of chance." Clark's dream of a "chic resort and a glamorous mecca for the rich and famous" was finally a reality. (*Las Vegas Sun Sunday Magazine*, May 29, 1979)

Flowers were everywhere, even around the figure-8 shaped pool. Clark, himself, stood in the middle of the lobby greeting guests and passing out flowers from a large Joshua tree placed in the lobby just for the grand opening.

Edgar Bergen and Charlie McCarthy, Vivian Blaine, the Donn Arden Dancers provided entertainment for the special night, along with the Desert Inn Orchestra conducted by Ray Noble.

Edgar Bergen and Charlie McCarthy were part of the opening night entertainment. Image courtesy of UNLV's Special Collections.

With an eye towards locals who still preferred the "Old West" in their attire, the local papers ran advertising for the grand opening that included, "Come as informally as you like. Remember, it's still the Old West even though you're in the glamorous setting of Wilbur Clark's Desert Inn."

Guests entered through the shady porch. Turning left would lead them to the Hotel Registration desk. Turning right would take them to the 80 x 60 foot windowless casino. The casino held five crap tables, three roulette wheels, four black jack tables, and seventy-five slot machines. Sixty people worked in the casino, and a full-service race book was also part of the gaming complex.

Two saloons graced the premises. One was a rawhide bar decorated with stylized steer heads and raw leather straps, which dominated the Celebrity Room Bar. The Lady Luck Bar, at 90 feet, was the longest bar in the state. It offered an innovative form of gambling actually embedded in the bar itself. Before each patron was a circle of numbers resembling a roulette wheel. A corresponding roulette wheel was displayed in the center of the bar area. On the wall, located above, was a nude figure representing Lady Luck. Every hour the wheel would spin and the patron whose light flashed would win the shower of silver dollars falling from the nude statue's hands.

A drugstore with a soda fountain, dress shops—including Fanny's, a chic and well-known lady's shop in Las Vegas—were also included. Owned by Fanny Voss, a good friend of Wilbur and Toni Clark's, Voss was determined to help make their hotel a success. K-RAM Radio broadcast from the grounds. There

The Lady Luck Bar at the Desert Inn. Image courtesy of Carey Burke.

were apparel shops, curio shops, and both a barber and a beauty shop. Clark wanted his guests to have all the comforts of home.

"A tremendous wood-burning fireplace, set corner wise, adds to the warmth, but in no way interrupts the view of the center patio and landscaped gardens through one entire glassed-in wall." gushed a writer for *Architect and Engineer*.

Beyond the casino was the coffee shop, a dining room that overlooked the pool, and the Painted Desert Room, the 450-seat showroom with hand-painted murals by Charles Cobelle.

The menus all featured western flora and fauna on their covers. A complete New York Steak dinner cost $5.75 while a hearty omelet and asparagus-tip breakfast was only $2.50.

The Painted Desert Room boasted a "band car" that mechanically whisked the orchestra on and off the stage in one motion. The lighting was soft and indirect and its lighting board for the stage performances cost $35,000 from Kliegl Brothers and tied into 10,000 different lighting effects.

The motel wings ringed the turquoise blue figure-8 pool with cabanas at the edge of the pool. Inner tubes provided for the guest's enjoyment all had Wilbur Clark's Desert Inn emblazoned on them. At the north end of the pool was the Kachina Doll Ranch with a daycare center staffed by a psychologist. The daycare center featured murals, also done by Cobelle, that taught lessons in good manners. There was a playground adjacent to keep the children occupied.

The pool at the Desert Inn was a gathering place for men and women. Image courtesy of the Nevada State Museum, Las Vegas.

The neon sign designed by Hermon Boernge. Image courtesy of the Boernge family.

The hotel rooms were decorated in Western motifs with individual touches. There was a series of "Hollywood Suites" which were spacious and lavish in design, and these suites offered a large living room and two separate bedrooms, private showers, and a patio. The room rate was $5.00 a night and up.

The famous neon sign, designed by Hermon Boernge, was made of sheet metal and seemed to grow organically as it ascended from the tower. In script it said "Wilbur Clark's Desert Inn." It immediately caught the traveler's eye. The cloud shape was captured in sheet metal and according to Alan Hess, "poised with perfect artificiality against the real clouds and real desert." At night, it was outlined in neon. Clark used this imagery on everything from matchbooks to other souvenirs in order to help promote his hotel.

By all accounts, the hotel was a success from the beginning. The first week's profits were said to have been in excess of $750,000 (in 1950 dollars). The first month's profit from the Celebrity Room Bar was over $90,000. The only part that didn't seem to work was the dining room/showroom that struggled with a $50,000 overhead. Clark was paying Edgar Bergen $25,000 a week to perform. (*Las Vegas Sun Sunday Magazine*, May 29, 1979)

Local attorney Paul Ralli wrote of Wilbur Clark:

> See him in his own Desert Inn. Watch him through an evening. He will talk
> to everybody. Let me repeat, he will talk to everybody and anybody … There
> is a family air about the Desert Inn. And every molecule of warmth in the
> air is directly attributable and traceable to the man whose name prefixes the
> hotel as a trade mark. You never speak of the Desert Inn—you speak of Wilbur
> Clark's Desert Inn and this is precisely what it is.
>
> Paul Ralli, *Viva Vegas*

Into this mythic era of Las Vegas history, a cloud appeared on the horizon. Senator Estes Kefauver was investigating organized crime and its influence on America. His crime hearings were all the rage and Kefauver was scheduled to conduct hearings in Las Vegas in 1950. Almost certain to be questioned were guys like Moe Dalitz. Kefauver arrived in town on November 15, 1950. After almost six months of hearings, the committee members were tired. Many of the high-profile casino owners, such as Dalitz that they had subpoenaed, left town rather than appear before the committee. Clark testified to the committee, saying that he was the president of the Desert Inn and recalled the financial problems that he faced a few years earlier in trying to build his dream resort. He told the committee about approaching Dalitz and his partners for the needed cash. Kevaufer and his committee only interviewed five other men, including Moe Sedway of the Flamingo and William Moore, now a member of the Nevada Tax Commission and executive director of the Hotel Last Frontier, before heading back out of town a little more than a day later.

While the Kefauver hearings had shed a bright light on illegal gambling and the men and organizations involved, many of the illegal operations that were going on throughout the country were closing down and moving to Nevada, especially Las Vegas, where they would not run afoul of the law as easily.

On September 4, 1951, singer Frank Sinatra made his Las Vegas debut in the Painted Desert Room. Sinatra's career had been on a decline since his vocal chords had hemorrhaged while performing at the famed Copacabana in 1950. His love life was all over the news with his divorce from his first wife, Nancy, and his affair with silver screen siren, Ava Gardner. Other up-and-coming young singers had replaced the one-time bobby-sox sensation in the eyes of young girls. He had been in Lake Tahoe prior to coming to Las Vegas and the news on the front page screamed that Sinatra had tried to commit suicide by taking sleeping pills. Sinatra quickly discounted the story by calling it a miscalculation in counting his pills. The movie magazines and columnists called it Ava-baiting. No one was sure if his Las Vegas engagement would be a success or not. (Mike Weatherford, *The First 100*)

Whether by accident or design, Sinatra eases along at the beginning, selling himself with clever gab and contrasting tunes, then he boffs with *I'm a Fool to Want You*, on which he collaborated. From there on he has his room wrapped up and neatly tied.

Las Vegas Sun, September 1951

So began a love affair between the singer and the Las Vegas Strip that would last another thirty-three years.

In November 1951, Clark started to build a $1 million dollar, 165-acre, eighteen-hole golf course and country club. Locals called it "Wilbur's Folly" and predicted that no one would want to play golf in the Nevada heat. Clark planned to prove them wrong. In 1953, he sponsored the Tournament of Champions, a professional charity golf event that brought golfers and celebrities from around the world to compete.

Wilbur Clark congratulates the winner of the Tournament of Champions. Image courtesy of UNLV's Special Collections.

With talented Gene Murphy taking charge of hotel publicity after Hank Greenspun's departure in 1950 (he went on to found the *Las Vegas Sun* newspaper), the tournament brought high rollers to the hotel. The proceeds went to the Damon Runyon Memorial Fund for Cancer Research, a charitable organization chaired by the then-powerful columnist, Walter Winchell. Golfers such as Sam Snead, Cary Middlecoff, Julius Boros and Jimmy Demaret came out to the Nevada sunshine to participate. The other hotels contributed $25,000 the first year.

Al Besselink won the first-place prize of $10,000 by shooting a 280 over the eighteen-hole championship course and the prize money was awarded in silver dollars. Gene Murphy helped turn the Tournament of Champions not only into a showcase for the Desert Inn, but for all of Las Vegas as well. The Tournament was soon receiving extensive national television coverage and Las Vegas, by extension, was receiving national exposure.

Newspaper man Bill Willard, who was a stringer for *Variety* magazine, reported on the Desert Inn for its first anniversary. Willard listed all the stars that had performed at the Desert Inn. Names included Ben Blue, the Ritz Brothers, Jimmy Durante, Pearl Bailey, and Billy Eckstine, and gave credit to Frank Sennes and Donn Arden, who designed and choreographed the floor shows.

The D.I., as it was becoming known, attracted many well-known and famous guests. Perhaps it was the opulence, perhaps it was the service—perhaps it was a bit of both. But guests in that era included: Duke and Duchess of Windsor, Winston Churchill, Adlai Stevenson, then-U.S. Senator John F. Kennedy, and former president, Harry Truman.

Performers who would grace the Painted Desert Room in the 1950s included Frank Sinatra, Ed Sullivan, Betty Hutton, Noel Coward, Chico, and Harpo Marx. The Mary Kaye Trio, often cited as the first major lounge act, would often play for ailing stars.

As more hotels began to be built on the Las Vegas Strip and challenge the D.I's reputation of opulence and fine service, the owners did what was necessary to keep up. When the D.I. debuted its new, larger swimming pool, the Last Frontier across the highway filled in its old roadside pool and built a heated one of AAU dimensions. They also included a subsurface observation room at the deep end and a deck-side bar. (*Harper Magazine*, Dick Pearce, 1955)

The Desert Inn replaced their original pool with one even bigger, only to have the Sands create a beauty of free-flow design large enough to float a cruiser. The Tropicana would ultimately counter with underwater Muzak.

In 1955, long-time Las Vegas gaming figure, Tony Cornero, who was in the process of building his dream resort, the Stardust, came into the D.I. one summer night in July. He was playing craps when he died of a massive heart attack. Dalitz and his other partners would end up owning Cornero's dream hotel.

Wilbur and Toni Clark
celebrate Christmas, 1958.
Image courtesy of the Hugh
Taylor Collection, Nevada
Preservation Foundation.

Wilbur Clark was a tireless ambassador not only for the hotel that bore his name, but for the city of Las Vegas as well. From his second-story office that overlooked the pool and was just below the Sky Room, Clark publicized his love for his hotel and his home on the radio, in newspapers, magazines, and on television. Wilbur and Toni Clark were one of the premiere couples in town.

Invitations to their home for dinner and/or drinks were some of the most sought after. After years of living in the small motel while trying to finance and build his dream resort, Clark pulled out all the stops when he had his home on the hotel's golf course built. It had an early security camera. Guests would ring the doorbell, and inside the home, Clark could see them on closed circuit television and talk to them.

An indoor pool that resembled the large pool at William Randolph Hearst's San Simeon graced the property. Clark had a personal tanning bed in his work-out room and the large living room had a fireplace in the middle so that entertaining was easy. It was a mid-century dream of a home with all the modern conveniences that money could afford.

Wilbur and Toni Clark traveled the country and the world promoting Las Vegas and Wilbur Clark's Desert Inn Hotel and Casino.

Image of the grounds of Wilbur Clark's Desert Inn, courtesy of the Nevada State Museum, Las Vegas.

But in 1956, Wilbur Clark suffered a stroke. A harbinger of things to come, the stroke forced Clark to slow down.

A KNIGHT NAMED HOWARD

The D.I. was considered to be the best in Las Vegas. Everyone was taught to talk to the guests and smile, whether winning or losing. You could just feel the warmth.

Security Chief Don Borax

In the early 1960s, the Desert Inn was keeping pace with all the new resorts that were opening on Highway 91, which was now becoming known as Las Vegas Boulevard South.

Keeping faith with the town and its growing population, in 1963, the Desert Inn went skyward and built a nine-story tower, the St. Andrews, complete with a high roller penthouse on the top floor. The Riviera had been the first hotel to be built with a tower and people had complained when it was being built that there would never be enough tourists coming to Las Vegas to fill it. Well, the Riviera proved everyone wrong and in the 1960s the majority of the original hotels on the Las Vegas Strip were remodeling and renovating to add hotel towers to their properties.

The iconic cactus neon sign was moved atop the new tower. The tower replaced the motel wings originally designed by Wayne McAllister.

Wilbur Clark, however, was being told by his doctors to slow down and curtail his activities. His poor health was getting the best of him, and Clark reluctantly sold his remaining interest in the hotel to Moe Dalitz, Morris Kleinman, and their associates, and retired in 1964.

Despite the loss of Clark, the Desert Inn management, under Dalitz, continued to make the hotel profitable. Rumors were rife that Dalitz and his partners regularly under-reported the money collected by the casino. This practice, better known as skimming, helped conceal the involvement of hidden outside investors who wanted to avoid paying taxes on the money collected.

Dalitz had the Painted Desert Room remodeled and renamed The Crystal Room. The showroom became home to one of Donn Arden's early revues, *Hello America!* Arden was busy trying out different story lines and dramatic pieces, including the sinking of the Titanic, and one day they all merged into the *Hallelujah Hollywood!* extravaganza at the original MGM Grand Hotel.

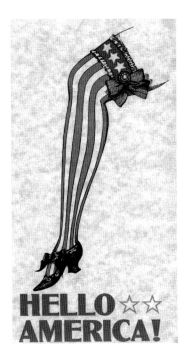

Souvenir program from Donn Arden's extravaganza *Hello America!* Image courtesy of UNLV's Special Collections.

By the middle of 1964, the Desert Inn was being advertised as a 272-acre resort with something for everyone.

A year after Clark's retirement, the Sky Room was once again remodeled, this time by the original designer, Jac Lessman. Hoping to accommodate more late evening dancers, a larger dance floor was installed. He added a new circular bar as well as a piano bar centered on a concert grand piano. Lessman also added two more rooms that could be rented for private parties.

An era was passing, however. Wilbur Clark died of a heart attack on August 27, 1965. The outpouring of love and grief was almost immediate. Clark had been responsible for bringing some of the biggest names in the world to Las Vegas, including the Duke and Duchess of Windsor. Clark and his wife had entertained world leaders at the D.I. over the years. Over 1,000 people turned out for the funeral. Honorary pallbearers included Senator Alan Bible, Senator Howard Cannon, Congressman Walter Baring, Governor Grant Sawyer, Lt. Governor Paul Laxalt, Attorney Harvey Dickerson, and Mayor Oran Gragson. Former Desert Inn publicist, now *Las Vegas Sun* publisher, Hank Greenspun, delivered the eulogy:

> Wilbur helped shape the character of Las Vegas. He was not looked upon as an exponent of the gaming industry but more as a Horatio Alger who walked half-way across a nation at a young age, practically penniless, to find his fame and fortune in the true tradition of the American Dream. Clark was a dreamer who could never keep pace with his dreams because he never stopped dreaming up to the moment of his death when he was continuing plans for a large string of hotels bearing his name across the country.

Entertainers who attended the services included Jimmy Durante, Sonny King, and Pepper Davis. Other local notables included Sheriff Ralph Lamb, the Sand's Jack Entratter and Carl Cohen, J. Kell Houssels, Milton Prell, Moe Dalitz, Chester Simms, Harley Harmon, Mahlon Brown, Sr., Major Riddle, Ben Goffstein, Ed Levinson, Art Ham, Sr., Sam Boyd, Merv Adelson, Irwin Molasky, Beldon Katleman, Jerry Mack, Stan Irwin, Ross Miller, G. William Coulthard, and former sheriff, W. E. "Butch" Leypoldt.

Yet the town was not prepared for the guest that quietly arrived on Thanksgiving Eve in 1966, nor the impact he would have on not only the Las Vegas Strip but Southern Nevada as well.

Arriving in Las Vegas via train and then transported to the Desert Inn via ambulance, Howard Hughes, frequent visitor to the "bright light city" in his younger days, returned to Las Vegas very quietly. Robert Maheu, Hughes' right-hand man had made arrangements with Moe Dalitz for Hughes to stay in the ninth-floor high-roller penthouse. Hughes' entourage took over the eighth

Howard Hughes. Image
courtesy of UNLV's Special
Collections.

floor of the hotel. Dalitz always claimed it was with the understanding that
Hughes would be out in time to accommodate the high-rollers expected between
Christmas Day and New Year's Eve.

Hughes, who was born Christmas Eve, 1905, had been coming to Las Vegas
since the 1940s. He would fly into town landing at either the Sky Haven Airport
out on the old Tonopah Highway (today North Las Vegas Airport) or at George
and Peg Crockett's Alamo Airways, located near where McCarran Airport is today.

Hughes was often seen dining and enjoying the shows at the El Rancho Vegas
and other Strip properties in those days. Longtime residents remember how
quiet and unassuming Hughes was back in the 1940s and how recognizable he
was in his tennis shoes.

He was seriously injured in an accident while testing an experimental, amphib-
ian plane over Lake Mead in 1943. In 1946, he crashed into a house in Beverly
Hills while test piloting his experimental plan, the XF-11. The crash left him
disfigured and addicted to prescription drugs for the rest of his life. Hughes had
been showing signs of obsessive compulsive disorder since the crash. In the late
1950s, he was diagnosed with neurosyphillis, a venereal disease that attacks the
brain. Symptoms included irritability, delusions, and carelessness about personal
hygiene and grooming, which plagued his later years. His fear of contamination
led to his insistence on living in a "germ-free zone." Hughes became reclusive in

the early 1960s when he moved into a highly guarded mansion in the wealthy Bel-Air section of Los Angeles along with wife, starlet Jean Peters, whom he had married in Tonopah, Nevada, in 1957. (Geoff Schumacher, *Howard Hughes: Power, Paranoia & Palace Intrigue*)

The settlement of a lawsuit with Trans World Airlines, which Hughes owned at one time, left him even wealthier. He received $500 million for his shares in the company. Not wanting to pay taxes on his windfall, he was ready to leave Bel-Air (leaving Peters behind) and had Maheu find him lodging in Las Vegas with the idea of "becoming the largest, single property owner in the gaming capital." (Jeff Burbank, *Online Nevada*)

Thus, Hughes arrived in Las Vegas on November 27, 1966. He was taken by stretcher via a service elevator to the Desert Inn's ninth-floor penthouse.

As the Christmas holidays drew near, Dalitz began to worry that Hughes would not leave in time for Dalitz to be able to accommodate the expected high-rollers. Dalitz told Maheu that it was time for Hughes to go. Maheu told Hughes that Dalitz wanted them out. Hughes told Maheu to buy the hotel.

Maheu asked for a price and Dalitz reportedly replied "$13.2 million" to buy the hotel. Though very over-inflated for its worth, Hughes paid the $13.2 million and became the owner the following spring. (Geoff Schumacher, *Howard Hughes: Power, Paranoia & Palace Intrigue*.)

Moe Dalitz, though not the owner of record, had gained majority control of the Desert Inn in 1949 when Wilbur Clark needed his financial help to finish building the hotel. Dalitz enjoyed the reputation around Las Vegas of being philanthropic and almost everyone tended to look the other way at reports that Dalitz under-reported the casino winnings and that skimming was a regular occurrence in the counting rooms. With Clark out of the picture, the FBI developed a very large interest in the way that Dalitz and his crew ran the hotel. Dalitz and the hotel were, more often than not, under FBI surveillance.

Did the government ask for Hughes's help in ridding Las Vegas of the mob? Much has been made of that, but the bottom line was that Hughes and his employees did not have any experience in running a successful hotel and casino and many of the same people who were loyal to Dalitz stayed on to work for Hughes, and they didn't necessarily change their counting habits.

Over the next two years, Hughes would also buy the Silver Slipper, the Frontier, the Castaways, the Landmark, and the Sands. He was attempting to buy the Stardust when the federal government finally stepped in due to monopoly and restraint of trade concerns.

In 1966, the last Tournament of Champions was played. Hughes did not see the importance of the tournament and though the event had done quite a bit to help promote not only the hotel but the town itself, it came to an end. The

Souvenir program for Donn Arden's
latest spectacle, *Pzazz! '68*.
Image courtesy of UNLV's Special
Collections.

purse had grown to $75,000 and the list of participants included Arnold Palmer, who won the Tournament that year.

As the 1960s music gave way from the traditional crooner to rock and roll and then pop rock, the Desert Inn hoped to stay current by hiring Tom Jones to headline the Crystal Room for two weeks. Connie Stevens, Jimmy Webb, and a host of younger names were soon added to the marquee. In addition, *Pzazz! '68* a new revue by Donn Arden, replaced the more wholesome *Hello America!*

Comedian Jerry Lewis also headlined during the late 1960s and was often chauffeured to Garwood Van's Musicland store where he would purchase sheet music and reminisce with the former bandleader who was also from Newark, New Jersey.

On Thanksgiving Eve, 1970, four years after he arrived and changed the face of the Las Vegas Strip forever, Howard Hughes left town as quietly and stealthily as he arrived. Robert Maheu had gotten into an argument with his boss and was fired just before the exodus. In the four years that Hughes had lived at the Desert Inn, he had never left his penthouse and was never seen by anyone but his closest aides. He was spirited away to the Bahamas and left his Las Vegas empire under the control of Bill Gay.

For the twentieth anniversary of the hotel on April 24, 1970, Edgar Bergen was invited back to the hotel to perform. Debbie Reynolds signed a million-dollar contract to appear at the resort through 1973. Louis Prima, Sam Butera and the Witnesses anchored the lounge.

The traditional idea of headlining a hotel had been that the performer was tied to the hotel that had hired him. Hughes, by owning so many properties, had made it possible for his headliners to play the other hotels under his banner. Robert Goulet signed a three-year, $3 million deal to appear at the Desert Inn, the Frontier, and the Sands.

Even though Howard Hughes passed away in 1976, the Desert Inn (and his other properties) remained part of the Summa—formerly Hughes Tool Company—Corporation.

Before Hughes died, he had authorized an expansion of the hotel. While not as opulent and expensive a renovation as Hughes had green-lit, the Summa Corporation did go ahead with the expansion. The fourteen-story Augusta Tower was built with an all-glass facade. The room total was now at 825, including suites. It was revealed in 1980, after Hughes had died and his estate filed a motion with the court,

> that the expansion was allegedly mismanaged, resulting in additional costs of $30 million. He [Bill Gay] never had a comprehensive plan for the construction. … Rather, it was constantly being changed, depending on his whim. … At one point, Gay decided that one of the new buildings, which already had been topped out, should have an extra floor, on which he planned plush suites for himself. The building was altered to add the additional floor at a cost in excess of $1 million.
>
> Geoff Schumacher, *Howard Hughes: Power, Paranoia & Palace Intrigue*

Burton Cohen was hired as general manager and would oversee the Desert Inn throughout the 1970s. Cohen had worked at many of the other resorts on the Strip, including the Frontier. He had been general manager there when Hughes had Robert Maheu call and complain about the light from the big neon sign keeping him awake. Cohen, who had worked for other stubborn visionaries including Jay Sarno, refused to turn off the sign. Hughes bought both resorts and had the sign turned off.

Cohen encouraged the filming of the television series *Vega$* on the property. Cohen figured it was good advertising to have star Robert Urich as private eye Dan Tanna showcasing the resort on one of the most popular weekly television shows on the air.

By 1978, the resort was advertising that most of the original 1950s structures were gone and had been replaced by more modern buildings. By the 1980s the

Desert Inn facade at dusk in the 1960s. Image courtesy of As We Knew It: Classic Las Vegas Collection.

hotel boasted an 18,000-foot spa, a championship Golf Course that included a driving range, pro shop, restaurant, and a cocktail lounge. Ten outdoor tennis courts were overseen by pro Marty Hennessy giving lessons to patrons. The Monte Carlo Room was a small, intimate restaurant. The Portofino Room was the Gourmet Room and sported modern glass and marble. Ho Wan was the Chinese restaurant located loft-like above the casino. The casino had 460 coin-operated gaming devices including traditional slots, video poker, 21, and Keno.

In 1985, to celebrate its thirty-fifth anniversary, a time capsule was buried on the property to be opened on April 24, 2020.

In 1986, the Summa Corporation sold the Desert Inn to Kirk Kerkorian. The sale was finalized in 1987 and for a while the resort was known as the MGM Desert Inn, though no one really called it that. It was still the D.I.

The PGA added the Desert Inn Golf Course to its Senior PGA tour which brought back many former players and winners of the Tournament of Champions.

By 1991, the Crystal Room had a rotating showcase of Frank Sinatra, Liza Minnelli, Willie Nelson, and Steve Lawrence and Eydie Gorme. The showroom was dark on Mondays and Tuesdays. Buddy Hackett decided to try an idea of appearing in the Crystal Room on Monday and Tuesday evenings without an orchestra or an opening act. Despite front-office skepticism, Hackett was a sell-out.

An advertising brochure for the Desert Inn. Image courtesy of UNLV's Special Collections.

The hotel was rebranded the Stars Desert Inn in 1992. But it didn't matter, no one called it that. It was still the D.I. to those that loved it. A smaller showroom, the Starlight Theater, opened. Another time capsule was buried on the property to honor Frank Sinatra's birthday. It was to be opened on Dec. 12, 2020. It is now, like the other one from 1995, buried under the Wynn Resort.

In 1993, the ITT-Sheraton Corporation purchased the resort from Kerkorian for $160 million. Almost immediately there was talk of plans for renovating. A private casino for high rollers was opened. Hoping to capitalize on the Desert Inn's reputation as a sanctuary for high rollers, the Sheraton offered a

$50 Sunday buffet that included three different types of caviar. The Starlight Theater's original location became part of the casino. The theater was moved to where the pool had been located and the pool was relocated to make it even more exotic.

Hoping to garner some of the classic Las Vegas glamour back, Keely Smith and Sam Butera were signed to play the new Starlight Theater. Though they hadn't worked together since the early 1960s, the duo was wonderful together, evoking memories of their days with Louis Prima, and their show became one of the hottest tickets in town.

On December 19, 1997, the grand opening of the $200 million expansion took place. Going for more luxury, the Sheraton had reduced the number of rooms from 821 to 715. Architects Tate and Snyder with Hirsch Bedner Interior Design Associates revamped the Augusta Tower.

The St. Andrews Tower was revamped by architect Paul Steedman. Steedman also oversaw the building of the nine-story Palm Tower. A Grand Lobby was completed as well as a new Golf Shop and Country Club. Both were overseen by Tate and Snyder.

In 1998, the Auto Club of America gave the resort a Four-Diamond rating as well as the Monte Carlo Room restaurant. The Monte Carlo Room was the only Four-Diamond restaurant in Nevada at the time.

But it was not to last. Starwood Hotels and Resorts bought ITT-Sheraton and acquired the Desert Inn in 1998. Starwood Chairman Barry Sternlicht put the resort on the auction block, because despite the high-priced renovation, the hotel was losing money.

Hoping to keep morale from plummeting among the employees, Starwood held an award ceremony honoring Employee of the Year Philip O'Reilly, the captain of the Monte Carlo Room. They also awarded a number of back-of-the-house employees as well as front-of-the-house employees. Keeping it all equal, management was honored as well.

Sun International Hotels agreed to buy the Desert Inn for $275 million cash in 1999. Sun, which operated hotels in the Bahamas, Atlantic City, and on the coast of the Indian Ocean, finally had a hotel in Las Vegas. Sun Chairman Sol Kerzner was likened to Mirage chairman, Steve Wynn, in numerous press releases.

Before they could take ownership, Kerzner and the other executives had to be investigated by the State Gaming Board. The closing was expected in the second quarter of 2000. There was talk of yet another renovation. The 715-room hotel now sat on 25 acres of prime Strip real estate. The deal also included the 140-acre Desert Inn Golf Course and Country Club Estates and another 32 acres of vacant land on the Strip south of the resort and along Sands Avenue across from the Venetian Hotel and the Sands Expo and Convention Center.

In 2000, the Desert Inn was fifty years old. She had survived numerous renovations and numerous owners. With the exception of Burton Cohen, none seemed to treat the hotel with the love and care that Wilbur Clark and Moe Dalitz had.

By March of 2000, Kerzner announced that Sun International was pulling out of the $275 million deal. Starwood immediately put the resort up for sale. There was a poison pill in the agreement. If the Desert Inn sold for less than $275 million, Sun would pay 50% of the difference up to $15 million.

The resort had a fiftieth birthday party that lasted a week from April 24-30. The festivities began with a celebrity golf tournament on the Desert Inn Golf Course, the last remaining eighteen-hole championship course on the Strip. A black-tie party in the Crystal Room that evening featured Lorna Luft in a tribute to her mother, one-time Las Vegas headliner, Judy Garland, and a fireworks display launched from the Golf Course.

Toni Clark, Wilbur's widow, and in failing health, sent a letter to the employees of the Desert Inn.

To My Dearest Friends,

It is with the greatest pleasure that I am able to write this letter to all of you. As I had done for many years at Wilbur's side, I would love to shake your hands, welcome you to our beautiful resort and thank you again for your patronage and friendship. Wilbur was a man of his word. When we married in 1944, he vowed to me a world of love and excitement, I must say my life was so very full of both. When he opened the Desert Inn, he promised the staff and guests an unparalleled, first class property. Again, he succeeded in keeping the promise. I must add that throughout the years, each group that managed the D.I. has gone to great lengths to maintain Wilbur's legacy of quality.

We were all so very proud to be a part of the Desert Inn in those days. And, I can see the same sense of pride and dignity with the people that work here now. The Desert Inn is an integral part of my heart and I can proudly say, my heart has never been broken.

April 24, 2000, is the Desert Inn's fiftieth birthday. I recall two remarkable grand openings a half century ago. My husband and I hosted a gala for VIPs and then a second function for the general public. They were both marvelous events. I can still to this day recall Wilbur's pride and magnificent smile that was so contagious for all of us. We had a marvelous time. The Desert Inn holds many memories and fulfilled dreams. It is my wish that our Desert Inn will continue to provide happiness and joy for you.

Toni Clark

To honor the occasion, a third time capsule was buried in a custom-designed granite burial chamber on April 25. Items placed in the capsule included the employee photo that appeared in *Life* Magazine, a recreation of that photo from 2000, a special section of the *Las Vegas Review Journal* commemorating the fifty years of the resort, a sales video, a television commercial, current menus, photographs of the resort, a security badge, and a media kit. It was to be opened on April 25, 2050.

On April 28, 2000, during the week-long birthday celebration, Steve Wynn bought the hotel for $270 million. Wynn and his wife, Elaine, were the only shareholders. Wynn said the resort was a birthday gift to his wife.

Today, the Wynn and its sister hotel Encore sit on the property that was once the Desert Inn and the Desert Inn Golf Course and Country Club Estates.

Wilbur Clark in front of a helicopter. Image courtesy of the Nevada State Museum, Las Vegas.

7

THE SAHARA HOTEL
1952-2011

FROM HUMBLE BEGINNINGS

For a place known more for its desert surrounding and the summer heat, post-World War II Las Vegas certainly looked very inviting to a certain breed of entrepreneur. Men with an eye towards the future were coming into town to build hotels that catered to people hungry to travel after the rationing, horrors, and sacrifices of the war. In less than ten years, there were five hotels—the El Rancho Vegas, Hotel Last Frontier, the Fabulous Flamingo, the Thunderbird, and Wilbur Clark's Desert Inn—built on the two-lane highway that led from Los Angeles to Fremont Street.

Though some locals wondered where all the people would come from to fill the new resorts, the men with vision kept assuring everyone they would come.

Frank Schivo was a long-time gambler who had the idea for the Club Bingo, a 300-seat bingo parlor. Like many before him, he had a dilemma: finding investors who would be willing to take the financial plunge. He lucked out when he met Milton Prell from Butte, Montana. Prell had operated the 30 Club in Butte, but, like many other gambling visionaries of the day, he relocated to the more legally friendly climes of Las Vegas in the 1940s. Though not as well known today as others such as Wilbur Clark and Del Webb, Prell nonetheless made an impact on Las Vegas. Club Bingo opened on a rainy day, July 24, 1947. In addition to the bingo parlor there were a few other games of chance. However, the Club Bingo had a reputation for fine food in its Bonanza Room. There were no hotel rooms—the Club Bingo was just a club for gambling and fine dining, and they had a small showroom that showcased the talented Dorothy Dandridge, comedian Stan Irwin, and the African-American swing group, the Treniers.

Milton Prell soon realized that the future of the Las Vegas Strip was in having a resort hotel that catered to the tourists swarming in from Southern California. That meant financing the building of a major hotel.

The Sahara Hotel had a North African motif. Image courtesy of the Nevada State Museum, Las Vegas.

The Club Bingo before Milton Prell had a better idea. Image courtesy of As We Knew It: Classic Las Vegas Collection.

Located on the east side of the Highway and directly across from the El Rancho Vegas, the Club Bingo had a prime location. In the years ahead, Prell would also build the Lucky Strike and the Mint Hotel on Fremont Street, but it was the construction of the Sahara that led to the creation of the Sahara-Nevada Corporation which he would ultimately sell to Del Webb.

Prell approached Dallas financial wizard A. Pollard Simon with plans for two-story hotel with 276 rooms. Simon agreed to go ahead with the Sahara project, despite the fact he was also helping finance Wilbur Clark's Desert Inn. Local air-conditioning contractor Al Wild introduced Prell to Del Webb. Wild had known Webb since the 1930s and Webb had just finished working on the Fabulous Flamingo. Prell and Simon agreed to a "cost plus" arrangement that included a percentage of hotel stock (20%, it was later learned) be given to Webb as partial payment for his services. (Jeff Burbank, *Online Nevada*)

The architect was Max Maltzmann and the designer was Albert Parvin. Maltzmann had been working in Los Angeles since the 1920s.

Architecturally, according to Alan Hess, "the Sahara followed the basic pattern of the Desert Inn and the Thunderbird. It featured a tall brick pylon at the

Photo souvenir jacket from the Congo Room. Image courtesy of As We Knew It: Classic Las Vegas Collection.

entry which anchored the low wings that spun outward from its center like a pinwheel." The motif was similar to the Arizona Biltmore in Phoenix designed by Frank Lloyd Wright. There the sculptural elements of the textile block provided ornament. At the Sahara, the signage became the ornament. (Alan Hess, *Viva Las Vegas: After-Hours Architecture*)

The theme was North African and evoked memories of the film classic *Casablanca* (1942) and other movies set in that exotic locale. Statues of plaster camels and nomads dotted the facade.

Inside there was the Congo Room (the showroom), the Casbar Lounge, and the Caravan Room. All that seemed to be missing was the Cafe Americain from the Academy Awarding-winning film. Life-size models of African warriors, spears held high, flanked the Congo Room entrance. A nomadic caravan including camels was placed out front on the lawn.

Like all the other hotels back then, the Sahara was basically a motel masquerading as a high-end resort. It had a low main building with a lobby and a casino in the front and the rooms to the sides. The glass restaurants such as the Caravan Room looked out not only on the pool area but the well-manicured and landscaped lawns. Author Lucius Beebe gushed that "its twenty acres of landscaped ground with rare blossoms and shrubs make even Boston's Public Gardens look to its tulips."

On September 18, 1952, the Nevada Gaming Commission granted gaming licenses to Milton Prell, Al Winter, and Barney Morris.

Originally set to open in the summer of 1952, the Sahara officially opened on October 7, 1952. Construction delays were the cause for pushing back the date. The headliner for the opening was Ray Bolger who had starred as the Scarecrow in the well-known pre-war film, *The Wizard of Oz*.

Stan Irwin was offered the job of Entertainment Director. Tired of being a comedian on the road, Irwin decided to take the offer. He had wanted Bolger—who had quite a success on Broadway with *Charley's Aunt*—to open the new hotel.

Irwin asked who had the most influence over Bolger and was told it was Mrs. Bolger. Irwin called Mrs. Bolger and explained that the Congo Room was not a nightclub but a showroom where Ray would be able to showcase his many talents. Ray Bolger agreed to open the Sahara.

Milton Prell dubbed the hotel the "Jewel of the Desert." Opening night was so successful that "the money had to be rushed straight from the cash boxes underneath the tables to the casino cage at a frantic pace so that guests could continue to cash in their winnings." (*Las Vegas Sun Sunday Magazine*, June 3, 1979)

Despite all the good fortune for its guests, the Sahara soon found itself in the same precarious situation that Cliff Jones and Marion Hicks had encountered when they opened the Thunderbird. The house was losing money and the guests

The front of the hotel in the late 1950s (note the billboard for Louis Prima and Keely Smith on the left). Image courtesy of the Nevada State Museum, Las Vegas.

were in danger of owning the property. Luckily, according to Stan Irwin, Milton Prell had planned for the occasion. He had called the other investors and gave them a heads up that they might need to wire money to keep the hotel solvent, just in case. Prell was prepared to put $5,000 of his own money into the till. The other investors agreed to do the same. Prell called them at the appointed time and the money was wired. Within the week the Sahara was making a profit and Prell returned the "emergency money" to each investor.

Though new to the job, Stan Irwin proved himself adept at booking the best in entertainment. Until the Sands opened and Jack Entratter began booking the Copa Room, Irwin was holding his own against the other entertainment directors in town. However, "Smilin' Jack" Entratter had started out in New York City and had booked the famed Copacabana for a number of years. He knew many of the stars of the day personally and that made him a formidable booking opponent.

Milton Prell decided to hire Bill Miller. Miller, like Entratter, had his roots back East. He had owned and operated the Riviera nightclub in Fort Lee, New Jersey. He had booked acts like Frank Sinatra, Dean Martin, The Will Mastin Trio, and others for years. In addition, Miller was an agent for crooners such as Tony Martin. However, a highway was going to be built that would go right through Bill Miller's beloved Riviera club. About that time, he got a phone call from Las Vegas.

"We'd love for you to come out and take a piece of this place, and be part of our group," Miller remembered Prell telling him. Miller bought a 10% interest in the property and was named Entertainment Director in 1953. (*Las Vegas Sun Sunday Magazine*, June 3, 1979)

Miller talked Mae West into headlining the Congo Room:

> I brought in people nobody believed could do a nightclub act," says Bill Miller, the man who virtually invented the Las Vegas lounge show. "For instance, do you think you could ever get Mae West to play in a nightclub? I did."
>
> K. J. Evans, *The First 100*

He found a group of spectacularly buff young men who looked good in swim trunks and hired them to accompany West onstage. They strutted and flexed and West leered. With her quick wit and sharp sense of timing, she was an immediate hit.

"I wrote her a song for the very finish," laughs Miller. "It went, 'I've got something for the girls: boys, boys, boys.'" (K. J. Evans, *The First 100*)

Miller hired Marlene Dietrich and people flocked to see a living legend in person, especially in the peek-a-boo dress that under the lights made it appear that Marlene was almost bare above the waist.

But Miller wanted to reshape lounge entertainment. He believed there was a way to make a lounge not only profitable, but if there was good entertainment late at night it might help bring more gamblers into the casino. The Mary Kaye Trio and the Treniers were anchoring the lounge at the El Rancho Vegas but that was about it for lounge entertainment in those early days. "It was basically a guy with a violin. The lounges were a joke. I said, 'This is ridiculous.' I've made all my money in show business selling whiskey. I can make more money selling whiskey than you can gambling." (K. J. Evans, *The First 100*)

Miller had been the agent for a bandleader/singer out of New Orleans named Louis Prima. In 1954, Prima called Miller looking for work.

> "How would you like a seven year deal?" Miller asked. Prima wasn't convinced when he heard he would be a lounge act. "You're going into the lounge, Louie," said Miller firmly. "You're going to be there seven years. You're going to live in the town and you're going to make more money than you ever did."
>
> K. J. Evans, *The First 100*

Miller offered Prima $3,500 a week and another $3,500 a week for his partner and wife, Keely Smith. Prima agreed to the deal. He and Keely Smith moved to Las Vegas just before Christmas. After a few nights of playing the Casbar Lounge, Prima knew their act wasn't working. Traditionally, the week between Christmas and New Years was a slow time but Prima was afraid that the hotel might cancel their contract if things didn't improve. He called an old friend and saxophone player in New Orleans. Sam Butera answered the phone on Christmas Eve. Louie offered to fly Butera and his band to Las Vegas to be part of the act. Butera hedged on leaving his family on Christmas so they agreed that Butera and the musicians would arrive on December 26.

The drummer and piano player barely had time to meet Prima and Smith before going on stage that night. Louis Prima introduced Keely Smith, Sam Butera and the Witnesses. The audience liked the name and it stuck. The lounge entertainers performed sets between midnight and 6:00 a.m., every night. They rotated generally with a comedian so that there was always entertainment in the lounge.

> And there was no one, ever, in the history of show business that did the business that this man did from midnight until 6 in the morning. You could not get into that club. That was really one of the biggest things that happened in Vegas, Miller recalled. It created people like Shecky Greene. All the lounge acts started with Louis Prima.
>
> K. J. Evans, *The First 100*

Keely Smith, Louis Prima, and Sam Butera and the Witnesses performing in the Casbar Lounge at the Sahara Hotel. Image courtesy of the Nevada State Museum, Las Vegas.

"We were the hottest act in the world!" recalled Sam Butera. (Interview with the author, 2003)

Prima, Smith, Butera and the Witnesses kept the joint jumping all night long. Performing five shows a night, three half-hour shows, and two forty-five minute shows, Prima and his group brought his raucous New Orleans-style of entertainment to Las Vegas and it made not only them famous, but the Sahara became the late night place to be.

Bill Miller's talents were soon evident to other hotel owners and offers began to come in. Miller decided to buy an interest in the new Dunes Hotel and became their entertainment director. To replace Miller, Prell hired Herb McDonald as the hotel's executive director of advertising, publicity, and promotion. McDonald and Stan Irwin were good friends, having arrived in Las Vegas about the same time. Though Miller had been the senior entertainment director, when he left for the Dunes, Irwin retained the title again.

Irwin, working with McDonald and his assistant, Harvey Diederich, arranged for an acrobat named Karl Carsony to do a one-arm handstand on a cane on top of the 50-foot tower pylon sign. They insured the acrobat with Lloyds of London for $100,000 and invited photographers everywhere to come and take a look. The stunt cost the hotel $400 and was worth thousands in publicity.

Also, they rented a billboard at the corner of Sunset Blvd. and Doheny on the famed Sunset Strip and had a miniature of the Sahara's Garden of Allah pool recreated. It wasn't enough that the billboard swimming pool was filled with water and lights highlighted the name of the hotel and who was appearing in the Congo Showroom, but Irwin hired eight young ladies to lounge by the pool during daylight hours. The stunt cost $30,000 but resulted in a million dollars worth of publicity. (Katherine Best and Katherine Hillyer, *Las Vegas: Playtown U.S.A.*)

Like the other properties, the Sahara was segregated. The African-American performers, even though they performed for white audiences, were forbidden to stay at the hotel, eat in the hotel restaurants, or be seen in the bars or casino area.

The Sahara provided trailers for their African-American performers, so the performers would have some place to be comfortable between shows.

In 1955, the Sahara opened its gourmet restaurant, The House of Lords. The motif was dark wood and deep reds, and the idea was that everyone would be treated like royalty.

In 1957, Herb McDonald introduced the Sahara Golf Invitational. Unlike the Desert Inn's Golf Course, the Sahara Golf Course was not located on the Sahara property, it was located off of Sunset Road and was called the Black Mountain Country Club. The purse for the tournament was $2,500. In 1958, the first live TV show from Las Vegas was aired on CBS to promote the Sahara Hotel. Strangely,

Rendering of the House of Lords Steak House. Image courtesy of As We Knew It: Classic Las Vegas Collection.

it was not filmed at the Sahara but at the recently shuttered Royal Nevada. The show featured acts that were performing at the Sahara.

The Sahara became the first hotel and casino to obtain funding from a local bank. Local bankers were very reluctant to give loans to hotel/casino owners, considering them too risky to consider. The Bank of Las Vegas, headed by Parry Thomas and Jerry Mack, however, didn't follow that philosophy and loaned Prell $1 million to build an additional 200 rooms.

The expansion began in 1959. Designed by Los Angeles architect Martin Stern, Jr., the expansion included a convention hall on the Sahara's north side as well as a 127-foot vertical roadside sign designed by the neon artists at YESCO. The new fourteen-story high-rise tower sat on the far side of the pool and was patterned with windows, balconies, and towers that imparted a dynamic, sculptural quality. Atop the sign was a time and temperature board highlighted by a semi-Arabic S on the very top. (Alan Hess, *Viva Las Vegas: After-Hours Architecture*)

Rounding out the year, Irwin managed a coup over Jack Entratter. Irwin was able to sign a brash young comic from back East to perform in the lounge, rotating with Prima, Smith, and Butera. The contract was for three years and Don Rickles signed on the dotted line. Irwin constructed a contract that was

The Sahara replaced their original roadside sign with a tall pylon sign in the 1960s. Image courtesy of the Nevada State Museum, Las Vegas.

well-used by performers. It contained a requirement for appearing at the Sahara for a minimum of twelve weeks a year with a stated salary. They could appear anywhere else the rest of the year using the Sahara salary as a basis to negotiate.

> I was playing the lounge there. Shecky Greene and I were the rival comedians at the hotel and I followed Louis Prima, who was the biggest thing in Las Vegas at the time. Shecky and I would do shows at 2 and 5 in the morning.
>
> Don Rickles in a 1992 interview

THE SWINGING SAHARA

Hollywood had made a few films featuring Strip hotels but M-G-M upped the ante on that when it was decided that *Ocean's Eleven* (1960) would be primarily shot on location. One of the hotels chosen as a location was the Sahara. This version, starring Frank Sinatra, Dean Martin, Sammy Davis, and a host of others, is a wonderful time capsule of what the Las Vegas Strip and the hotels in this era looked like.

The Kingham family enjoying a show in the Sahara's showroom, the Congo Room. Image courtesy of As We Knew It: Classic Las Vegas Collection.

Dancer Eleanor Powell returned to the stage for the first time in fourteen years on Feb. 28, 1961. Stan Irwin had worked hard to get her to sign the contract and Powell reportedly rehearsed six hours a day, six days a week. She insisted on auditioning for Milton Prell as well. She worked hard and her return to the stage was a success. It was noted that Powell's show received more press coverage than any other before her.

In 1961, Prell sold the Sahara to Del Webb. Webb merged his construction company with the Sahara-Nevada Corporation and became the first publicly traded company to have holdings in a Las Vegas gaming establishment. Also included in the deal were The Mint and the Lucky Strike Club. Frank Schivo, whose idea it had been for the Club Bingo and who had worked there from the beginning, was promoted from casino manager to vice-president. Prell stayed on until 1964, when he moved to Southern California to pursue an investment opportunity in Beverly Hills.

With the merger completed, Webb had enough money to do a $12 million facelift on the hotel. On February 9, 1962, groundbreaking ceremonies were held for the new twenty-four-story tower that would add 400 rooms to the resort. In addition, Webb wanted to expand the casino space and add a 1,000-seat convention hall, and new dining and gaming areas. There would be two additional swimming pools also added.

Hotel Sahara Main Lobby

DESIGNED FOR GUEST COMFORT—Ready for use July 1, this spacious new main lobby of Hotel Sahara is set off with a deep rich color scheme of reds, oranges and blacks, complimented with minor accents of brass. Candled bulbs in decorative brass lighting fixtures highlight the colorful stationary seating units, brass inlaid formica tables and the woven carpet that is finished in a stained glass effect. Featured adjacent to the lobby will be escalator service to the second floor Convention Hall, hotel executive offices and the landing to the third floor Don the Beachcomber restaurant.

The Sahara's Main Lobby gets a makeover in this rendering. Image courtesy of As We Knew It: Classic Las Vegas Collection.

As part of the renovation/facelift, the main lobby was reconfigured and designed for guest comfort. It was done in a rich color scheme of reds, oranges, and blacks complimented with minor accents of brass. The woven carpet had a stained glass effect and the furniture was considered colorful. An escalator led to the second floor Convention Hall, Executive Offices, and then up to the third floor where the Polynesian-themed Don the Beachcomber would be located. The restaurant was slated to open on September 1, but was delayed until the following year.

A Keno parlor was added. This was only the second Keno game on the Strip at the time. Keno was a big draw on Fremont Street and the visionaries on the Strip had taken note. The Sahara had a $25,000 Keno game and added 550 slot machines to their casino. Malacca teak was highlighted throughout the casino.

The Caravan Room was redone featuring a pleasing combination of gold tiles and smooth gold surfaces, lending the coffee shop a hoped-for majestic quality. Individual booths situated on the circumference of the room featured floating grillwork while one of the two service stations islands was decorated in the same grillwork with a floating canopy. The wooden blinds and subdued lighting highlighted the "golden touch in dining," according to publicity material from the hotel.

The House of Lords was set in regal red tones with notes of black and deep wood paneling. Pewter and stained glass fixtures highlighted an intimate English atmosphere while heavily carved wood beams and an inlaid wood ceiling, finished in Malacca teak, provided a distinguished background for dining pleasure. The barbecue area sparkled with a stainless steel counter, while the bar area, finished in used brick with accents of red velvet, added a reserved touch of dignity to the royal setting. Sinatra, Martin, and the Rat Pack had loved the original House of Lords and were often late-night diners after they finished their shows at the Sands.

Bad news came in October 1961. Louis Prima and Keely Smith were divorcing and breaking up their incredibly successful act. Smith would go on to have a solo career, and Prima, Butera and the Witnesses continued to work together. Prima married Gia Maione in 1962 and she would join the group, replacing Smith, but the group that had done so much to create the lounge scene in Las Vegas would never regain that initial popularity.

The comics that Bill Miller and Stan Irwin had hired helped keep the lounge jumping even with the loss of Prima, Smith, and Butera. Shecky Greene was performing in the Casbar Lounge one evening and felt like nothing was working. He laid down on the stage, stared up into the lights, and went on with his act. Buddy Hackett and Victor Borge were in the audience and joined him on stage. The audience went wild. (Mike Weatherford, *Cult Vegas*.)

Elvis Presley was often spotted at the hotel. Colonel Parker and Presley were both friends of Prell. Elvis enjoyed the lounge bands, especially Freddie Bell and the Bellboys.

According to Bell, Presley would come into the lounge and sit in the back and enjoy the show. He didn't like to be pointed out to the audience but he did enjoy Bell's impression of Presley. Presley and Bell had become friendly when Presley had performed at the Hotel Last Frontier in the 1950s. Bell and his group, the Bellboys, were one of the better-known lounge acts, and Presley heard Bell singing "Hound Dog." Presley would cover the song and make it a number one hit.

In 1962, the hotel opened a new restaurant called Don the Beachcomber, a Polynesian-style eatery that was part of the tiki trend then sweeping the nation.

A new promotion, the *Shower of Money*, was planned and became quite successful. The winning ticket holder was showered with $100,000 in U.S. dollars and given one minute to grab the bills. The smallest denomination was $5. The winners kept all the cash they could grab. If they were guests of the hotel they received an additional $100 bonus.

On February 10, 1964, a testimonial dinner was held to honor Milton Prell. Prell was retiring as president of the Sahara-Nevada Corporation (soon to be renamed the Del Webb Corp.) and moving to Southern California. He would retain the title of chairman of the board.

Freddie Bell and the Bellboys performing in lounge. Image courtesy of UNLV's Special Collections.

Don the Beachcomber logo. Image courtesy of As We Knew It: Classic Las Vegas Collection.

Stan Irwin hired late-night talk show host, Johnny Carson, to play the Congo Room in July 1964. Reservations flooded in from all over the country. Carson set a new record at the hotel, with the Congo Room filled to capacity throughout his two-week stay.

But the Sahara's biggest coup was for a group that due to ticket demand would not be able to play the Sahara. Stan Irwin and Herb McDonald hatched a plan to bring The Beatles to Las Vegas. Irwin had heard through his Hollywood connections that the Beatles wanted to play Las Vegas, but none of the hotels approached so far saw the big picture. Irwin and McDonald did. The Beatles were the hottest group in the country and Irwin figured that teenagers would want to see the mop-top boys from England. What he hadn't expected was the overwhelming response from customers in Southern California. Reservations flooded in.

Irwin knew that the Congo Room was not big enough to hold the screaming masses of teenagers clamoring to see the Beatles, so he made arrangements for them to stay at the Sahara, but perform two shows at the nearby Las Vegas Convention Center. The Rotunda normally sat 7,000. Irwin reconfigured the seating to accommodate 8,408 people per show.

The Beatles were booked to perform on August 20, 1964, at 4:30 and 7:30 p.m. The top ticket price was $25. The Las Vegas Convention Center marquee read: "The Sahara Hotel and Stan Irwin present: The Beatles."

About a week before the show, the other hotel owners and entertainment directors began calling to see if there were any tickets left. The high rollers were coming to town and bringing their children, nieces, and nephews who all wanted to see the lads from Liverpool.

Stan Irwin remembered in a 2005 interview with author, "that I could have charged $1,000 per ticket and likely still sold out but I wasn't brought up that way."

Irwin made arrangements for the plane to land at McCarran Airport. Two limos with police escort were there to escort the lads to the Sahara. Teenagers laid siege to the hotel, trying to get a glimpse or touch their favorite Beatle. Irwin had planned carefully for the Beatles to leave via the back entrance of the hotel and be taken to the Convention Center. When it came time for the group to come down, the back entrance was swamped with hundreds of young people. Security, News Bureau photographers, and Irwin all locked arms and made a path for the Beatles to dash to the waiting limos.

Two acts opened for the Beatles. When the band from Liverpool finally took the stage among the screams of hysterical teenaged fans, they played a 45-minute set.

Between shows, they were whisked back to their suites at the Sahara.

The Beatles flew out of Las Vegas at 2:00 a.m. The irony of the situation was the reason they wanted to play Las Vegas was because they wanted to see the

The Beatles performing at the Las Vegas Convention Center on August 20, 1964. They stayed at the Sahara Hotel during their very short visit. Image courtesy of Bo Boisvert.

town and be tourists. All they really saw was the inside of the limos, their hotel suites, and the Convention Center.

On August 25, 1964, a fire swept across the roof of the main casino. It was extinguished in about forty minutes, but water damage forced the main casino, the Casbar Lounge, and the Congo Room showroom to be closed for repairs. The showroom was relocated upstairs in the convention facility while the damage was repaired.

The Congo Room reopened on October 1, 1964. President Lyndon B. Johnson visited the resort in October and stayed overnight in Del Webb's suite.

Irwin made an offer of $75,000 to Colonel Parker for Elvis to play the Sahara. The Colonel, unfortunately, said no.

From his beginning as the house comedian at the Club Bingo to reinventing entertainment on the Strip, Stan Irwin now felt it was time to move on. He gave Del Webb his letter of resignation, effective August 15, 1965. Irwin had brought a number of stars to the Sahara and had his share of firsts. He was the first entertainment director to do away with a Master of Ceremonies and turn the showroom into more of a theatrical evening than a nightclub. He was the first to put two names on the bill at the same time. He was the first show producer to spotlight a Late, Late Show (2:30 a.m.) with a headliner that was different than the one who performed at the dinner or late show. Irwin had trail-blazed this idea by hiring Judy Garland. He knew that Garland would have trouble doing two shows every night at 8:00 and 11:30, but she was dynamite, given that she was a night owl, at 2:30 a.m.

Among the other stars he had hired: Morey Amsterdam, Ray Anthony, Eve Arden, Tony Bennett, Ray Bolger, Victor Borge, Teresa Brewer, George Burns, Johnny Carson, The Characters, The Crosby Brothers, Marlene Dietrich, Shelley Berman and Sergio Franchi, Connie Francis, Robert Goulet, Betty Hutton, Fernando Lamas, Steve Lawrence and Eydie Gorme, Donald O'Connor and Irene Ryan, Jane Powell, Don Rickles—who went from the lounge to the Congo Room after subbing for an ill Johnny Carson and brought the house down—Phil Silvers, Kay Starr, and The Beatles.

In 1967, the Convention facility at the Sahara got not only a facelift, but a makeover. When the renovations were completed it was now 44,000 square feet of convention space and put the hotel at the forefront of the convention business. Built at cost of $3.5 million, one of the unique features was that it had no internal support columns to obstruct display space.

Dubbed the "Sahara Space Center" (this was, after all, the era of the Space Race), the facility became home to the *Jerry Lewis Muscular Dystrophy Telethon*. Traditionally, Lewis had done the live telecast from New York City with satellite feeds from Los Angeles and Las Vegas. But by the early 1970s, Lewis realized that it was easier to get the high-end entertainers, especially in the wee hours of the morning, if they could stop by after they were done with their late show. Las Vegas in that era was home to some of the best entertainment in the world.

The Strip marquees from Sahara Avenue out to the Hacienda boasted names such as Sinatra, Davis, Martin, Minnelli, Berle, Burns, Carson, the Smothers Brothers, Rickles, Diller, and more.

The lounge scene was still jumping with Louis Prima, Sam Butera and the Witnesses still in town, the Mary Kaye Trio, Pete Barbutti, Shecky Greene, and more. It was easier for those stars not appearing on the Strip to come to Las Vegas from Los Angeles for the telethon than it was for them to fly to New York City.

The move revitalized the Muscular Dystrophy Telethon and every Labor Day weekend the Sahara reaped the publicity. It also helped that the out-of-town stars usually stayed at the Sahara as well. In those days, the Strip was primarily designed for the automobile instead of the walker's paradise it is today. Back then there were wide swaths of empty desert between the properties and many stars such as Steve Allen, Marty Allen, and his wife, Frenchy, Telly Savalas, Sonny and Cher, and others found it more convenient to stay at the hotel. This made the weekend great for celebrity sightings for tourists also staying at the hotel.

A woman in a fur coat places a bet on the roulette wheel. Back then, people dressed up to go to a hotel. Image courtesy of UNLV's Special Collections.

The Sahara boasted a state-of-the-art PBX switchboard that was rumored to house $250,000 worth of equipment. The hotel employed twenty switchboard operators who handled, on average, 5,000 calls a day. This was in addition to paging customers—"Miss Virginia Slim, white courtesy phone please"—taking messages for guests, making wake-up calls, placing long-distance calls, and acting as hotel ambassadors.

It was that era of non-stop entertainment where everyone enjoyed the round-the-clock atmosphere. Back then there weren't many places that stayed up 24/7, so that gave Las Vegas a certain cachet. People were amazed to discover they could get their hair cut in the middle of the night, have breakfast any time they wanted, and there was no final call.

The entertainers were mainly household names thanks to long careers in the movies, radio, television, and record sales. Variety shows were popular on television and seeing Dean Martin or Bing Crosby on a variety show made you want to see them in person on stage in Las Vegas. The showrooms were small, intimate rooms—standard seating was 450-650 per showroom—and the sound systems were top of the line. The musicians in the various hotel orchestras were some of the finest players in the world.

Going to see a show in Las Vegas meant getting dressed up in an evening gown and wearing your best jewelry. For men, it meant dusting off that tux or black suit and finding a good tie. It was a wonderful era where the party was never supposed to end.

But, as the 1960s progressed, that all started to change with the coming of Howard Hughes and corporations. For a few, swinging years, though, Las Vegas enjoyed being America's Adult Playground and the Sahara Hotel was in the thick of that playground.

THE 1970S AND BEYOND

From its humble beginnings as the Club Bingo to its rollicking history of the 1960s, the Sahara Hotel had made a name for itself up and down the famed boulevard.

Milton Prell had the vision and had hired the right people to make that vision a reality. As the 1960s wound down, Del Webb had overseen the growth of the resort. By the early 1970s, the property was being described as a 20-acre oasis, located at the start of the famed Las Vegas Strip. It boasted 1,000 luxurious

The Sahara Hotel in the 1970s. Image courtesy of the Nevada State Museum, Las Vegas.

During the Muscular Dystrophy Telethon in 1976, Frank Sinatra orchestrated the reunion of former partners, Dean Martin and Jerry Lewis. The once-renown comedy duo had been estranged for almost 20 years. Image courtesy of UNLV's Special Collections.

rooms and suites, all with television and radio. There was the twenty-four-story skyscraper and the fourteen-story Sahara Tower. Three pools, a fashion gallery, health club, five restaurants, nine bars, an airline ticket office, and complete convention facilities helped make the hotel feel like a miniature city.

In 1976, the Space Center again played home to the *Jerry Lewis Muscular Dystrophy Telethon*. It was the usual star-studded event. This year, however, was made more memorable by a gesture of Francis Albert Sinatra, the Chairman of the Board. He reunited Dean Martin and Jerry Lewis, former partners who had been estranged for nearly twenty years.

"You been working?" Lewis asked his former partner and friend, Dean Martin.

"Yeah, I got a few weeks at the MGM Grand," Martin replied with a twinkle in his eye.

The two men embraced and when Martin walked off-stage, Lewis told the audience, "That was my former partner." By all accounts, the reunion helped Martin and Lewis to rekindle their friendship before Martin's untimely death years later. The Telethon took in a record high that year: $21,723,813.

In 1977, the Sahara renovated the Space Center by completely recarpeting and repainting. They also upgraded 300 rooms and forty suites. The Casbar, home to many rollicking nights in the 1950s when Louis Prima, Keely Smith, and Sam Butera were rocking the joint, was closed and renovated, as was the Caravan Room.

In 1979, under the direction of Vice-President and General Manager R. Edward Zike and Del Webb Corporate Vice-President Ed Nigro, construction began on a $50 million expansion program that was touted as one of the most extensive in Las Vegas history.

The expansion included a 3,000-car parking lot and security towers across Paradise Road with a fully lighted lot. It was all connected to the back entrance of the hotel by an overhead, air-conditioned walkway. A new *porte cochere* was built for the back entrance with the idea that it might become the new entrance some day. And, as always, another hotel room tower was planned. This tower would be thirty-seven-stories tall and house 625 rooms. The building was, briefly, the tallest building in Nevada. The top two floors would be a two-story penthouse with spiral staircases.

In 1982, the Del Webb Corporation sold the Sahara Hotel to Paul and Sue Lowden for $50 million. Adjusting to the changing musical tastes of the country, the showroom at the Sahara now featured such acts as Alice Cooper, Ricky Nelson, Jerry Lee Lewis, and a former lounge singer turned headliner, Miss Tina Turner. Comedians included Redd Foxx and Don Rickles.

But bigger changes were coming. In 1989, Steve Wynn opened the Mirage Hotel, and in 1993, opened Treasure Island. The hotels quickly ushered in a new era for the Las Vegas Strip. The older hotels had to compete with new properties that appealed to a younger crowd. While locals and the older generation still enjoyed places like the Sahara and the Stardust, the winds of change were apparent up and down the boulevard. Trying to keep up, the Lowdens added another twenty-six-story tower before selling the property to Bill Bennett in 1995.

Bennett oversaw the renovation of the hotel in 1996 and again in 1999. The 1999 renovation included the Speedworld addition and the Nascar branding.

Bennett died in 2003, leaving the hotel (and the land across the street where the El Rancho Vegas once stood) to his family. While the hotel seemed to be holding its own, its age was apparent and its days of overflowing crowds were behind it.

In 2007, the Bennett family sold the hotel (but not the parking lot property on Paradise Road) to SBE Entertainment Group and Stockbridge Real Estate Funds. As the face of the northern end of the Strip began to change with the building of Steve Wynn's Encore Hotel, the Sahara seemed to be running on fumes.

The Sahara Hotel closed for good on May 16, 2011. The fixtures were auctioned off and SBE chief executive Sam Nazarian stated that the "hotel was not as economically viable as it was." SBE Entertainment put the hotel through a rigorous makeover and rebranded the property the SLS Hotel and Casino.

It opened in August 2014, and has struggled to find its audience.

Letters from the Sahara's pylon sign in the Neon Museum's Boneyard. Image courtesy of As We Knew It: Classic Las Vegas Collection.

8

THE SANDS HOTEL
1952-1996

THE PLACE IN THE SUN

The Sands Hotel, perhaps more than any other popular resort, came to symbolize the Las Vegas of our collective memory. It was here that the color line for entertainers staying at the hotel was finally broken. It was here that Frank Sinatra, Dean Martin, and Sammy Davis, Jr., and the rest of the Rat Pack held court in the Copa Room.

Sinatra, Martin, and Davis were the hottest tickets in town, and it was at The Sands Hotel that John Kennedy visited during a campaign trip through Southern Nevada. Glamour and glitz, politicos and power mongers all met in the desert, and it helped propel tourism to this small desert oasis like no other.

Originally, there was a small French restaurant called La Rue's on Highway 91 (the old LA Highway). It was owned by Nola Hahn and Billy Wilkerson, creator and one-time owner of the Fabulous Flamingo (see chapter four for more details on Wilkerson).

Jake Freedman, an oilman from Texas with a penchant for western attire and pretty girls, and Mack Kufferman wanted to build a new hotel on the burgeoning Las Vegas Strip. They bought the land where La Rue's sat and set about to build a resort that would cater to both the high rollers and the Hollywood glamour crowd. Others rumored to be financing the building of the resort were organized crime figures Meyer Lansky, Frank Costello, and Joseph "Doc" Stracher, as well as illegal bookmakers Ed Levinson, Syd Wyman, and Michael Shapiro.

Freedman hired Los Angeles architect Wayne McAllister, who had also designed the El Rancho Vegas, to create the resort. In 1940, McAllister worked closely with owner Tommy Hull of The El Rancho Vegas to create a modern day version of the Old West. Since then, McAllister and his partner, William Wagner, had been working in Los Angeles designing upscale restaurants such as Lawry's Prime Rib.

The original Sands Hotel, a Place in the Sun. Image courtesy of the Nevada State Museum, Las Vegas.

Instead of going for a western or southwest motif as the other hotels along the highway were doing, McAllister wanted to bring a mid-century modern look to the Sands Hotel. Jake Freedman gave him a free hand and did not interfere with the design. The result, according to author Alan Hess, was the "most elegant piece of architecture the Strip had ever seen." (Alan Hess, *Viva Las Vegas: After-Hours Architecture*.)

Freedman originally wanted to call the resort the *Holiday Inn* after the Bing Crosby/Fred Astaire musical, but serendipity had other plans. One day while visiting the site, Freedman was approached by one of the hotel's builders, who told him that a working name for the hotel was needed and asked Freedman for a name. Freedman looked around and replied, "There's so much sand in this damned place that my socks are full of it! So, why don't we call it 'The Sand' until it's finished and then we'll call it the 'Holiday Inn.'" When the builder pointed out that the name should be plural, "The Sands," Freedman reluctantly agreed. (*Las Vegas Sun Sunday Magazine*, June 17, 1979)

Once Freedman realized that people preferred "The Sands" over his own choice, he decided to go with the popular choice.

The original exterior of the Sands Hotel, designed by Wayne McAllister. Image courtesy of the Nevada State Museum, Las Vegas.

Sands Hotel owner Jake Freedman with the Copa Girls. Image courtesy of The Sands Collection, UNLV's Special Collections.

The resort would have 200 rooms and a casino, and cost $5.5 million to build. The look of the hotel would be dramatic and modern. Instead of tearing down La Rue's, McAllister kept the building. Its location on the street dictated that the Sands be located close to the highway. McAllister, according to biographer Chris Nichols, would have preferred the hotel to set further back for easier car access but he soon made the location work for him.

> The flat-roofed casino was large, perhaps the largest built to that date. McAllister designed an eye-catching *porte cochere* and a zig-zag wall ornamented with tiled planters along the sidewalk to off-set the cavernous mass of the structure.
>
> Atop the *porte cochere* were three sharp-edged beams that jutted out from the building and flowed over the glass-walled entry before angling down into the ground, giving the appearance of fins. The two-story glass-walled entry was bordered by a monstrous sheath of marble. A horizontal plane with can lights and suspended from the beams sheltered guests as they arrived.
>
> Alan Hess, *Viva Las Vegas: After-Hours Architecture*

Along the circular drive, metal sculptures, columns, and stucco pylons created a screen between the entry and the gardens. Four two-story motel wings, named after famous American racetracks, each with fifty rooms, stretched back on the property and surrounded the half-moon shaped pool. The structures featured unique vermiculite tile roofs, which were used extensively in the tropics to provide cooler temperatures.

Hotel guests were transported from the hotel to their rooms via electric trams. Inside, "the main building of the Sands is a great rectangular hall, with the reception desk in one corner, slot machines along one long wall and a bar and cocktail lounge, complete with a musical Latin trio to keep the mood lively, along the opposite wall. In the middle is a jumble of roulette and craps tables and twenty-one layouts," wrote A. J. Leibling in the *New Yorker* in 1953.

Three large terrazzo stairs led into the large casino, as lighting was provided by low, modern-looking chandeliers. Along the walls, signs marked the Copa Room and the restaurants. Apart from the casino was a bar featuring a bas-relief, stylized mural of galloping wagons, buttes, Joshua trees, and cowboys. Skylights illuminated the Garden Room restaurant.

Jutting out of the east side of the main building was a popular gathering spot called the Sunrise Terrace, which offered an unobstructed, stunning vista of Sunrise Mountain.

The crowning glory, though, was the roadside sign. It was a departure from the usual sheet metal and neon displays that beckoned road-weary travelers to stop and stay.

Guests were whisked to their rooms via the Sands trolley. Image courtesy of The Sands Collection, UNLV's Special Collections.

McAllister designed a 56-foot sign—the *S* alone was 36-feet-tall—by far the tallest on the highway at that time. With its elegant modern script, the sign blended with the building to create a mid-century modern paradise. The sign, which was fabricated by YESCO, and the building, had motifs common to both. With its egg crate grill, cantilevered from a solid pylon, The Sands' illuminated logo played with desert light and shadow like Lady Luck and a pouch full of 'C' notes. In bold free script, it proclaimed "Sands" in neon across the face. At night, it glowed red with neon spelling out the name. (Alan Hess, *Viva Las Vegas: After-Hours Architecture*)

A secondary, smaller sign stood by the southern highway entrance. Later, an attraction board was added to the main sign listing the headliners who were playing the Copa Room. Las Vegas had not seen anything quite like the Sands.

The Nevada Tax Commission, then the state agency that regulated casinos, threw a monkey wrench into Freedman and Kufferman's plans for the new resort. After a long investigation, the Commission refused to give either man a gaming license because Kufferman was linked to "Doc" Stracher, a known New Jersey mobster, and Freedman was linked to Kufferman. Freedman was a well-known international gambler and race-horse operator with Texas connections.

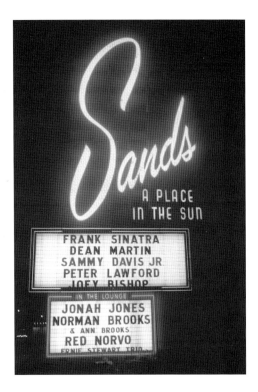

The Sands Hotel's neon sign at night. Image courtesy of the The Sands Collection, UNLV's Special Collections.

Freedman's partnership with Kufferman was the only reason the Commission denied his application. Freedman bought Kufferman out and was able to be licensed. However, the rumors of hidden mob money continued to swirl around the Sands throughout the 1950s and 1960s.

"Jakie Freedman was accepted and respected as a quality gaming operator," Sands executive Carl Cohen recounted in a 1979 interview. "He was known as a good host and a man of unquestioned integrity." (*Las Vegas Sun Sunday Magazine*, June 17, 1979)

Jake Freedman brought Jack Entratter west to work at the Sands. Entratter booked the famed Copacabana Room in New York City and had ties to most of the talent that traveled the nightclub circuit back East. Known to his friends as "Smilin' Jack", he was a mountain of a man, standing over 6'1". But he knew talent and how to negotiate. Under his leadership, the Sands quickly became known as "New York's Copacabana Gone West" featuring Lena Horne and Noel Coward. He spirited Marlene Dietrich away from the Sahara and Frank Sinatra away from the Desert Inn. The Sands had deep pockets and was willing to spend top dollar for good performers.

"Smiling Jack" Entratter (on
the left) and Jake Freedman.
Image courtesy of The Sands
Collection, UNLV's Special
Collections.

The pay rate for playing Las Vegas was astronomical considering it was the
1950s. Rates of $25,000 a week—usually for two to three weeks, two shows a
night, six days a week, and one on Sunday—were the norm. In 1955, Liberace
would command $50,000 a week from the Riviera. Most contracts had a min-
imum of weeks that had to be played throughout the year, ensuring that the
headliner played Vegas frequently. As Las Vegas gained in popularity, gamblers,
especially the high rollers, began traveling there instead of gambling in the back
rooms of nightclubs. The nightclubs across the country soon realized that they
could not keep up with Las Vegas pay days.

The Sands Hotel opened on Dec. 15, 1952. Danny Thomas, singer/songwriter
Jimmy McHugh, and the Copa Girls, "the most beautiful girls in the world,"
opened the famed Copa Room.

Ray Sinatra and his Orchestra were the house musicians, and the Copa Room
had seating for 395, featuring a series of nine sculptured metal Brazilian carnival
figures on the walls.

By the second night of his two-week run, Thomas, overwhelmed by all the
press coverage and unaccustomed to such attention, had strained his voice and
his doctor told him to take the night off if he wanted to be able to continue his gig.

A call went out and, in that old standard of Hollywood and Broadway, the show went on starring a hastily gathered group that included Jimmy Durante, the Ritz Brothers, Frankie Laine, Jane Powell, and Ray Anthony. It was, by press accounts of the evening, a wild, free-wheeling ad-libbed show that brought the house down. All the performers would ultimately play the Strip throughout the 1950s.

The success of the evening was captured by journalist Bill Willard:

> The Sands pulled out $50,000 from the vaults to stage a hunk of promotion surpassing the palmy days of P. T. Barnum. All ingredients were tossed into the flack salad, including four openings in one and all covered by reps of the press, radio, TV and pix.
>
> *Variety*, Dec. 1952

Freedman had hired Al Freeman as Head of Publicity. It was a strategic move that would pay off for years as Freeman wooed Louella Parsons, Bob Considine, and Earl Wilson to broadcast their radio shows from the Sands a few times a year. He invited atomic scientists and doctors to stay at the Sands during the atomic bomb tests that were routinely going off in the early morning desert skies above Yucca Flats. He wooed celebrities, dignitaries, and politicians. He worked closely with the photographers at the Las Vegas News Bureau to keep the Sands in the forefront of publicity. *Guys and Dolls* was a smash on Broadway and one of the favorite songs from the musical concerned a floating crap game.

True to the madcap spirit of the day, Freeman put a craps table in the pool. Don English, of the Las Vegas News Bureau, snapped the photograph of gamblers in swimming suits and Hawaiian shirts playing craps in the pool. The photo garnered international attention. Freeman was a master at his job and raised the bar for all the other publicity directors in town.

Back in those days, for a hotel, the money was made on the gambling and the cost of talent was the cost of doing business. Gamblers, especially the high rollers, would bring their wives, girlfriends, or mistresses to Las Vegas, and while the men were busy betting fortunes at the tables, the ladies were busy enjoying the shows, the shopping, and the celebrity watching. Entratter was instrumental in luring wealthy gamblers from the Northeast to come visit the Sands.

Women in low-cut gowns were at the craps tables and women in furs stood at slot machines hoping to win enough to brag about back home while their husbands and boyfriends did the real gambling at the tables.

Entratter and company were so good at promoting the Sands that it is said the hotel made back its original $5.5 million investment in the first six months. Rather than encourage the stars to play the tables, though it often attracted big crowds, Entratter encouraged them to deal. He figured if they lost big at the

The famous "floating craps table" photo taken by Las Vegas News Bureau photographer Don English. Image courtesy of Don English.

tables, they would blame the hotel and not perform there again. With them dealing instead of gambling, there would be no hard feelings. People flocked to the Sands in hopes of seeing a headliner dealing 21.

In 1953, the Nevada Tax Commission denied Frank Sinatra's application for a 2% interest in the hotel.

That same year, Entratter signed Tallulah Bankhead to play the Sands, offering her $20,000 a week. Pundits proclaimed that Entratter was crazy and would fall on his face with such an offbeat booking. Even Bankhead herself wasn't sure she would be any good. She, however, turned out to be a smash. *Variety* critic Joe Schoenfeld wrote, "Bankhead was bank night for the Sands Hotel."

A female gambler tries her luck at the craps table at the Sands. Image courtesy of The Sands Collection, UNLV's Special Collections.

Jack Entratter was successful in spiriting Frank Sinatra away from Wilbur Clark's Desert Inn and signed him to play the Copa Room. It was one of those miracles of timing, the right man at the right time in the right room. Sinatra, who just a few years previously had been considered washed-up, began his comeback to stardom on the stage of Copa. He had, by most accounts, a great deal of respect for Entratter who had continued to book him back East when he was in his washed-up stage and Sinatra was always grateful for that.

As the staff began planning the hotel's first anniversary celebration in Dec. 1953, Entratter ordered a 12-foot time capsule. Bankhead, who was headlining the Copa Room, helped publicize the burial. Inside the capsule was a headshot of Bankhead, Bing Crosby's pipe, Ray Bolger's dancing shoes, Sugar Ray Robinson's boxing gloves, a wax impression of Jimmy Durante's nose, an autographed copy of *Short'n Bread* sheet music by Nelson Eddy, and a transcript of Louella Parsons interviewing Sinatra on her radio program.

Celebration for the first
Sands Hotel anniversary.
Image courtesy of The
Sands Collection, UNLV's
Special Collections.

The capsule, in the shape of a rocket, was then lowered in the ground not to be opened for 100 years. Ten years after it was buried, the capsule was discovered in the landfill in nearby North Las Vegas near the pig farm. While rummaging through the landfill, filled with china plates and broken dishes, a family found Ray Bolger's dancing shoes. It is believed that while construction was going on for the 1963 expansion, the capsule was inadvertently dug up and thrown out.

In April 1955, Danny Thomas' brother was killed in a traffic mishap outside of Barstow. He was on his way to Las Vegas to see Thomas perform. Thomas was unable to go on so Sinatra flew in to cover for him. When Sinatra had to leave a few days later due to contractual obligations, Billy Gray took his place. Entratter's assistant, Nick Kelly, arranged for a special Memoriam Mass at local St. Anne's Church for Thomas' brother.

Fitness specialist Jack La Lanne's exercise program was all the rage in the 1950s and Entratter didn't miss a chance to grab some headlines for the hotel. It was announced that a Health Club, complete with Steam Room, would be built and it would be located directly off the pool.

While Entratter had an aggressive—and envied—booking policy, he didn't hit a home run every time. In 1955, he paired opera singer Robert Merrill and Louis Armstrong in the Copa Room. It was the first and last time.

Celebrities, it seems, loved the Sands. Humphrey Bogart and Lauren Bacall, Yul Brynner, Kirk Douglas, Rosalind Russell, Ethel Merman, Elizabeth Taylor, and more were photographed sitting in King's Row (the prized middle seats in front of the stage) enjoying the headliners performing onstage in the Copa Room.

The yearly anniversary parties were one of the hottest tickets in town. Those who headlined throughout the year would be there and often join Danny Thomas onstage. You never knew who would show up. The Anniversary celebrations were filmed by the Las Vegas News Bureau and were star-studded events.

Thomas, the star of the hit television show *Make Room for Daddy*, arranged to film episodes of his weekly show on the grounds of the Sands. His television family can be seen exploring the grounds of the property while "Daddy" is rehearsing his show in the Copa Room. Also, Thomas and his co-star, Marjorie Lord, filmed commercials for Maxwell House, the show's sponsor, at the Sands.

Nat King Cole was hired to play the Copa Room. Like other African-American performers, Cole had a trailer on the property because he was not allowed to stay in the hotel.

Nat King Cole on stage with the Copa Girls. Image courtesy of The Sands Collection, UNLV's Special Collections.

By 1955, Cole was tired of his trailer. He enjoyed performing at the hotel but he did not like the segregation policy that forced him to eat in the trailer between shows and now that he had a family, forced him and his family to drive to the Westside each night to stay in a boarding house. He told Entratter if he couldn't stay in the hotel he wouldn't perform at the hotel.

Sinatra was performing at the hotel and was, by now, a close friend of "Smilin' Jack's." He reminded Entratter that it wasn't just a problem with Nat King Cole, but for performers like Lena Horne and Sinatra's good friend, Sammy Davis, as well. Sinatra urged Entratter to break the color line. In 1955, with no fan-fare and no publicity, Entratter quietly allowed the headlining African-American performers performing at the Sands to stay there as well. (Jeff Burbank, *Online Nevada*)

As the 1950s continued, rock and roll began to catch on as a new and popular form of music. The Silver Queen Lounge at the Sands catered to both the emerging rock and roll crowd and the more American Songbook standards that were still very popular. Roberta Linn and the Melodaires rotated with Freddie Bell and the Bellboys and Gene Vincent.

In the mid-1950s, Ray Sinatra was replaced as Orchestra Bandleader by Antonio Morelli. Morelli's wife, Helen, was an advertising executive, and she had to remain at her job in the East until her contract was up. Once her contract was completed, she joined her husband in Las Vegas, and he set about designing a home for them on the Desert Inn Country Club Estates.

On January 20, 1958, Jake Freedman died following surgery to repair a blockage in his aorta. His wife Sadie was given a suite in the Belmont Park wing where she lived until she, too, passed away ten years later. Jack Entratter became president of the Sands Hotel. To help Mrs. Freedman pay her husband's gambling debts, Sinatra purchased a percentage of the hotel. By now an Academy Award-winning actor who was filling the town with tourists, Sinatra was finally licensed by the Nevada Tax Commission. He did not, however, take part in managing the hotel. That, he wisely left to Entratter.

The 1950s were coming to an end. The Sands had been responsible for bringing more glamour and more celebrities to Las Vegas than any other hotel. With their powerhouse line-up, they were the hottest hotel in town. Huge changes in The Sands' future were ahead in the 1960s, but before that happened, there was history to be made on the stage of the Copa Room for a month in 1960.

The famous Copa Room, the showroom at the Sands Hotel. Image courtesy of the Nevada State Museum, Las Vegas.

A PARTY EVERY NIGHT

In 1960, Frank Sinatra's production company, Dorchester Productions, agreed to produce a comedy heist film called *Ocean's Eleven*. It was to star Sinatra, Dean Martin, Sammy Davis, Joey Bishop, Peter Lawford, and Angie Dickinson. Hollywood veteran Lewis Milestone was hired as director. The story involved a group of World War II buddies robbing five Las Vegas Hotels on New Year's Eve. Sinatra suggested filming on location in Las Vegas. Thus, the Sands became the base camp for the cast and crew at the hotel.

For three weeks, from January 26 until February 16, the Rat Pack as they were known, filmed their scenes during the day, retired to the Steam Room for a few hours and then took the stage in the Copa Room for two shows nightly. It was known as *The Summit at the Sands*, and it quickly became the hottest ticket in town.

Audiences were never sure just who would be taking the stage each night, and if the rest of the Rat Pack would be there as well, and the mystery only added to the excitement. The Dinner Show at 8:00 p.m. was the tamer of the two nightly performances. Though it seemed as if the boys were ad-libbing their way through the evening, in reality, Joey Bishop was writing most of the material. The bar cart was wheeled on stage, and for the next two hours, the audience was never sure

Frank Sinatra, Peter Lawford, and Joey Bishop exit the stage during one of the performances of the The Summit at the Sands. Image courtesy of the Sands Collection, UNLV's Special Collections.

of what would happen next. Film footage reveals the five popular entertainers at the top of their game. Sinatra's album, *Songs for Young Lovers*, had become the soundtrack for the era. Martin proved that he was funnier than his reputation as a straight man for former partner Jerry Lewis had led people to believe. Davis provided the double whammy of singer and dancer.

"It was the greatest time of my life," Joey Bishop remembered "There was only one bad thing about it, though. I was in the first scene to be shot in the mornings while everyone else slept in." (*Las Vegas Sun Sunday Magazine*, June 17, 1979)

After the dinner show, they would have a break and then take the stage for the more raucous Late Show. Shirley MacLaine had agreed to do a small role in the film just so she could hang out with the Pack in Las Vegas. Celebrities poured into town to see the freewheeling, seltzer-spraying shows.

It was one of those defining moments in pop culture and the combination of Las Vegas and the Rat Pack was fused into the country's psyche. They would all play the Copa Room throughout the 1960s as single acts but the enduring memory remains of all of them onstage during the *Summit*.

From left, Peter Lawford, Frank Sinatra, Dean Martin, and Joey Bishop on stage in the Copa Room. Image courtesy of UNLV's Special Collections.

After the Late Show, the Pack would retire to the lounge where they would continue drinking and watch the entertainment such as comedian Dave Burton. They would often take the stage and clown with him.

> "Back then," Dave Burton recalled, "the lounge had a very long stage that was somewhat removed from the audience. Now, in the back there was the V.I.P. table reserved for the Rat Pack. I liked to con Frank, Dean, Sammy and the rest into coming up and joining my show. So I'd take my microphone with its long cord, down to Sinatra's table and do my songs from there, coaxing them up on stage. Frank liked to do physical humor, such as throwing ice at you while you were performing."
>
> *Las Vegas Sun Sunday Magazine*, June 7, 1979

Then they would retire for the night, catch some sleep, and start all over.

The publicity the *Summit* provided the Sands was priceless. When *Ocean's Eleven* was released later that year, the Sands figured prominently in the movie. Reviews of the film were generally good as many of the reviewers focused on the camaraderie of the stars and box-office returns indicate that the film was quite successful.

In May 1961, Jack Entratter's wife, Dorothy, passed away after a brief illness. Entratter poured himself into his work even more. A few years after his wife's death, he married a young Copa dancer, Corinne Cole.

In mid-1963, the Sands opened the Aqueduct wing, a three-story building containing eighty-three rooms and suites.

In September, Sinatra's gaming license came under scrutiny from the Gaming Control Board. Sam Giancana, a well-known Chicago mobster, had been seen staying at Sinatra's Cal-Neva Lodge in Lake Tahoe. Giancana was in the notorious Black Book, the list of excluded people who were not allowed in casinos, even as customers. Sinatra surrendered his license and had to also sell his interest in the Cal-Neva and his interest in the Sands.

President Kennedy stopped in Las Vegas on Sept. 28, 1963, to give a speech at the Las Vegas Convention Center.

The President stopped by the Sands to say hello to Sinatra. Two months later, President Kennedy was killed in Dallas and the hotel owners, like others, dimmed their lights in tribute.

In 1964, director Billy Wilder began filming *Kiss Me Stupid*, starring Dean Martin, with scenes filmed at the Sands Hotel. For the film, not only did the

President John F. Kennedy and Jack Entratter. Image courtesy of the Nevada State Museum, Las Vegas.

marquee have Dino on the attraction board, but a color caricature in neon and lights of Martin as well.

By 1965, the face of the Las Vegas Strip was changing yet again. Hotels were undergoing costly, almost yearly renovations to keep up with the visitors who were streaming into town for the great shows and the gambling. The Sands Hotel was no different.

In a nod to progress, they hired architect Martin Stern, Jr., to design a new high-rise tower that would replace their original building. This new seventeen-story tower would be a larger footprint than the original building and require that the hotel wings be moved further back on the property. The Wayne McAllister design of the original building was, according to author Alan Hess, remodeled into a plainer, less elegant facade with a new triangular *porte cochere*. This new *porte cochere* would be a free-form canopy supported by a single thin pylon.

Stern, like McAllister, was based in Los Angeles, and like many area architects had been a sketch artist at a movie studio back in the 1930s. He had apprenticed with Paul Revere Williams and William Gage. By the 1950s, he was a successful architect and designing housing tracts, apartments, and coffee shops. His "Ships" coffee shops in Westwood and Culver City were icons of Los Angeles "Googie" architecture, and like McAllister, Stern contributed to the highly stylized and popular roadside style of architecture with its bold shapes and modern imagery.

To keep the public's eye on the Sands while it was being renovated, the hotel hosted the National Automobile Dealers Association Convention. As part of the convention, a Buick was hoisted high in the sky above the hotel. Entratter also had a publicity plan for the Copa Room as well.

He signed Count Basie and his Orchestra to a two-week engagement with Frank Sinatra, and the hip new bandleader for Basie at that time was a young Quincy Jones. More than 75,000 reservations flooded into the hotel for the show, more reservations than there were seats. Based on the success of the reservations, plans were made to tape a live album featuring all the talent. *Sinatra at the Sands with the Count Basie Orchestra* would be one of Reprise Records' biggest selling albums. If you ever want to get a taste of what one of Sinatra's shows were like, this is the album to listen to.

The Copa Lounge got a makeover and became the Celebrity Theater. Opening headliners included Joe E. Lewis, Keely Smith, and Sonny King, and by the winter of 1965, Martin Stern's seventeen-story tower was opened. With fanciful arches across the crown of the hotel and new flicker-bulb signage atop the hotel, the tower was ready for business.

In July 1966, Sinatra approached Entratter with a dilemma. Sinatra was in love with a young starlet, Mia Farrow, and wanted to marry her, and Sinatra knew that it would turn into a media circus if not handled properly. Having been through the media burn years earlier when he had divorced his wife Nancy

Architect Martin Stern's concept rendering for the new Sands tower. Image courtesy of the Sands Collection, UNLV's Special Collections.

for Ava Gardner, he didn't want to relive that experience. Though he was single at the time, the age difference between the entertainer and the young star of television's popular nighttime soap opera, *Peyton Place*, was enough to raise eyebrows and cause another media clamor. Could Entratter help?

Entratter immediately said "Yes!" and Sinatra and Farrow were quietly married by a Justice of the Peace at the hotel, presumably in Sinatra's penthouse suite on July 19, 1966. Afterwards the newlyweds met the press for pictures and then were whisked away for their honeymoon.

Later that year, the singer hosted a star-studded 25th Anniversary Party for his friend, actress Rosalind Russell, and her husband, producer Freddie Brisson. The lavish affair was attended by the old guard of Hollywood royalty, everyone from Jimmy and Gloria Stewart to Cary Grant and reigning Hollywood stars such as Kirk Douglas.

Frank Sinatra and Mia Farrow get married at the Sands Hotel. Image courtesy of Bo Boisvert.

Entratter also signed Louis Prima, his wife Gia Maione, and Sam Butera and the Witnesses to a long-term, $1 million contract to play the Celebrity Theater. Though not as groundbreaking or as popular a show as it had been at the Sahara's Casbar when Keely Smith was with the group, the chemistry between Prima and Butera kept the audiences lining up for more.

Howard Hughes had come to Las Vegas on Thanksgiving eve, 1966, and by the end of that year had bought the Desert Inn Hotel. On July 22, 1967, his offer to buy the Sands Hotel was accepted.

For fifteen years, the Sands Hotel had the reputation as the best hotel on the famed Las Vegas Strip. Hotel management had hoped that no one would notice the change of ownership and the good times would keep rolling on. That seemed possible until the wee hours one September morning. Sinatra, by many accounts, had been drinking steadily all night. He had a large line of credit with the hotel courtesy of his friendship with Entratter who had been the president of the hotel for many years.

When Sinatra's line of credit ran out, he asked for an increase, which soon turned into a large demand. Sinatra continued to be turned down. Furious, he went looking for manager Carl Cohen. Cohen was in a booth in the Garden

Room coffee shop when Sinatra found him. Cohen tried to calm him down, but Sinatra threw a chair at Cohen. Cohen, in return, punched Sinatra in the mouth, dislodging his two front caps.

Sinatra, enraged, walked away. He returned a short time later and drove a golf cart through one of the lobby's plate glass windows, then headed to the airport, and flew back to Los Angeles.

The next day Sinatra signed a multi-year deal to headline Caesars Palace. Law enforcement was unable to get Sinatra's statement about the melee with Cohen. Cohen was more than happy to give them his side of the story.

The carefully built myth of the Sands Hotel being Sinatra's private playground and the myth of Sinatra being a caring and all-around great guy came crashing down with that plate glass window. Press accounts were filled with statements from long-time employees regarding Sinatra's ego, his reluctance to tip and his less-than-generous attitude to any staff member that wasn't a gorgeous Copa Girl or cocktail waitress.

Despite the chairman of the board's falling out with the hotel, Dean Martin continued to play the hotel until his contract ran out. He moved over to the Riviera and then he got a better offer from the newly built, original MGM Grand Hotel. Sammy Davis honored his contract until its end and then joined Sinatra at Caesars.

In 1970, Sinatra got into an argument with hotel executive Sanford Waterman. Waterman pulled a gun on the belligerent singer who was demanding more casino credit. Sheriff Ralph Lamb threatened to throw Sinatra in jail and was quoted, "I'm tired of the way he has been acting around here anyway." (Mike Weatherford, *The First 100*)

Sinatra, unaccustomed perhaps to not getting his way, was quoted as saying, "If the public officials who seek newspaper exposure by harassing me and other entertainers don't get off my back, it is of little importance to me if I ever play Las Vegas again." (Mike Weatherford, The First 100)

On March 11, 1971, Jack Entratter, who had become the heart and soul of the hotel after Jake Freedman's death, passed away. The town was stunned. "Jack Entratter was more than a friend, more than a boss. He was like a father to me and he will be greatly missed," said a grief stricken Sammy Davis, Jr. (*Las Vegas Sun Sunday Magazine*, June 7, 1979)

An era was coming to an end.

Jack and Entratter and
Sammy Davis, Jr. Image
courtesy of UNLV's Special
Collections.

AN INGLORIOUS END

Jack Entratter was gone.

The Summa Corporation, formerly the Hughes Corp., in a move that fore-shadowed the direction the Las Vegas Strip would go, tapped Richard Danner, a lawyer from Washington D.C., to replace the beloved Entratter.

Danner knew enough to keep the stable of performers that Entratter had signed. Robert Goulet signed a three-year, $3 million contract that included performing at other Hughes properties such as the Desert Inn and the Frontier, in addition to the Sands.

Wayne Newton, dubbed the Midnight Idol, was also performing at the various Hughes properties and was keeping the showrooms packed. He played an unheard of seven weeks straight at one point.

In May of 1976, the Sands made the news for the wrong reasons. Federal Judge Roger D. Foley had quashed a subpoena for the Sands to turn over all credit records on wealthy Saudi Arabian businessman Adnan Khashoggi. Khashoggi was an internationally known figure who had ties from London to Hollywood to Las Vegas and beyond. He was currently involved in a scandal involving

Jack Entratter. Image courtesy of the Sands Collection, UNLV's Special Collections.

The Sands Hotel, Showplace of the Stars. Image courtesy of As We Knew It: Classic Las Vegas Collection.

American aircraft manufacturing firms and foreign countries. The subpoena had been delivered to Richard Danner who told Foley that he had not been given enough notice to appear in court.

Khashoggi had flown out of the country on March 4 to apparently avoid testifying in the bribery scandal. Before he fled though, he had stayed at the Sands Hotel. Old-timers say he took over twenty rooms and was rumored to have spent thousands of dollars during the one-week stay. The government wanted the records to see whom Khashoggi associated with, how he made arrangements for his credit, and what transactions he had undertaken and completed before hopping on his private Boeing 727 and flying out of the country.

The Sands, ultimately, turned the records over to the federal government.

Howard Hughes had left Las Vegas in 1970 as mysteriously as he had arrived. In 1976, word came that Hughes had died while enroute to a Houston medical center from the Bahamas. Stories began circulating almost immediately about the poor condition the recluse had been in. Stories of an emaciated Hughes with long fingernails and a scraggly beard led the nightly news. The less sensational part of the story was just as sad. Bill Gay, a long-time Hughes executive and Chester Davis, Hughes' lawyer, had successfully driven a wedge between Hughes and his former right-hand man, Bob Maheu. With Maheu out of the picture, they began to isolate Hughes even further, while increasing not only their control over the reclusive millionaire but their pocketbooks as well. As there was no will, a struggle over the Hughes fortune soon erupted. Hughes' cousin, Will Lummis, ultimately took control of the estate, ousted Gay and Davis and the other members of the "Palace Guard."

The Hughes estate filed a motion with the court in 1980 alleging:

> These individuals ... are charged with having seized control of Hughes' empire and having enriched themselves at Hughes' expense. They are alleged to have done so, in large measure, by taking advantage of Hughes' drug addiction, seclusion and mental incompetency to run Hughes' enterprises—ostensibly in his name, but in fact for their own personal benefit—and by manipulating and controlling a virtually helpless Hughes.
>
> Geoff Schumacher, *Howard Hughes: Power, Paranoia & Palace Intrigue*

While the struggle over the Hughes estate continued, the Sands Hotel management tried to keep the hotel running. In 1977, the management proposed a golf course. Jack Nicklaus was to design the course, which would be a championship eighteen-hole course on 160 acres of land that would zig-zag behind the property. The 160 acres was owned by Hughes, but the course was never built, and the land was later used for what became the Hughes Center, a complex of offices, condos, and retail.

In February 1978, the Sands buried another time capsule. This one was to be opened in a more timely fashion, twenty-five years. It included medallions from Wayne Newton and Sammy Davis. Jimmy Durante and Sonny King donated the pairs of trousers they had both worn the last time they worked together, prior to Durante's retirement in 1970. Roy Clark contributed a monogrammed handkerchief, and then-President Jimmy Carter donated a bag of peanuts from his peanut farm in Georgia. The family that had found the 1953 capsule in the landfill contacted the Sands in the days leading up to the burial. They re-donated Ray Bolger's dancing shoes for the new time capsule. The family preferred to keep all the other original items.

Mayor Bill Briare donated a box of international messages from other officials, Triple Crown winner Seattle Slew's owners donated the winning silks, and NY Yankees manager Billy Martin donated an autographed Yankees ball. Like the time capsules at the Desert Inn, this, too, has been lost to history.

The casino floor of the Sands Hotel circa the 1960s. Image courtesy of the Nevada State Museum, Las Vegas.

In another example of how the times had changed, in May 1978, Sands slot manager, Peter Goin, Sr., was arrested for embezzling $171,000 from the hotel over a period of nine years. It was discovered that he had been paying himself $450 jackpots twice a week. Attorney Oscar Goodman was hired as his lawyer as Goin was charged with four counts of embezzlement, four counts of forgery, and four counts of tax evasion.

Goin tried to take Sheriff Ralph Lamb down with him. The two had been friends on the rodeo circuit and Goin claimed to have lent Lamb $10,000 without a promissory note. Lamb was later found innocent of tax evasion charges. Old-timers remarked how much times had changed by noting that if Goin had done that in the 1950s and early 1960s, the "boys" would have handled the situation much differently.

The struggle over Hughes' fortune came to Las Vegas. Hughes' cousin, William Lummis, had been named executor of the estate, and it took some time for him to get a handle on all of Hughes' holdings. Also adding to the problem were long-time employees that had helped themselves to parts of Hughes' fortune by setting themselves up with lifetime work contracts complete with high wages.

William Lummis advised the Summa Corporation to sell the casino properties and concentrate on more profitable pieces of the estate such as the many land holdings that Hughes had purchased. Lummis was determined that the Hughes Estate not be bankrupted by the under-performing casinos and some of the aircraft holdings.

Summa entered into a deal with the Inns of the Americas, a Texas-based company, in December of 1980. On May 1, 1981, it became official, and the Sands Hotel was sold for $85 million.

The new owners began a $15 million renovation. The Copa Room was closed for renovation on June 24, 1981. Governor Robert List read a proclamation from the stage that declared the day Copa Room Day in Nevada.

The renovations were completed in January of 1982. Local high school bands entertained the crowd. Sands favorite, Sonny King was the master of ceremonies and Sammy Davis was the special guest. Davis pulled the switch lighting up the new marquee, the Sands tower, and the new *porte cochere*. Over 200,000 balloons were released from the roof of the hotel, and a fireworks show completed the grand opening festivities.

Inside, the casino had also been remodeled. It was now over 30,000 square feet, twice the size it had been. An invitation-only dinner honoring Davis was held in the main ballroom and featured Harry James and his Orchestra.

The Baccarat room was now done in Italian marble and called the Casino Internationale. There were over 1,500 linear feet of neon throughout the casino.

The new marquee and *porte cochere* with the remodeled tower. Image courtesy of the Nevada State Museum, Las Vegas.

The new Copa Room was opened on March 17, 1982. Heralding back to its roots, Danny Thomas and ten Copa Girls took to the stage. Thomas proved that sometimes the old ways are the best ways and that you could go home again. While Thomas was on stage, it was easy to imagine that it was still 1952, and the Sands had her whole future in front of her.

In May 1983, Summa had to step in and re-take control of the hotel. The new owners had had high hopes for the Latin market, but when the Mexican economy nosedived, it left the hotel holding bad markers.

Summa kept the property until Kirk Kerkorian bought it in 1988 and he renamed it the MGM Sands. Kerkorian was only involved for a short while. The Interface Group, known for creating the computer and electronics Comdex convention, purchased the property from Kerkorian for $110 million. The deal was finalized a year later.

The changing face of the Strip was becoming apparent with the opening of Treasure Island and the Mirage. The era of the mega-resort was on the horizon and the Sands property was seen as aging and unhip by the new, younger crowd coming to town.

A 1.2 million square foot Convention facility, the Sands Expo and Convention Center, was built to try and capitalize on the burgeoning convention business. In 1993, new owner Sheldon Adelson announced a series of improvements. Changes included another 14,000 square feet of casino space, upgrades to the restaurants including replacing the Chinese restaurant with a coffee shop, and making the original coffee shop the buffet. A Race and Sports Book was enlarged and relocated to be closer to the showroom. More slot machines were added, but it wasn't enough. The bottom line was that the hotel just couldn't compete with the new resorts rising on the Strip. The Interface Group shareholders were bought out by Sheldon Adelson, and Adelson finally sold the Comdex Convention for $865 million.

Adelson toyed with the idea of bringing the Sands back to its original footprint and building a modern resort. Unfortunately, none of the plans for doing that appealed to him. He announced the hotel was closing and would be imploded.

The Sands officially closed on June 20, 1996.

Preservationists and entertainers implored Adelson to save the Copa Room. They had hoped he would turn it into a museum depicting the Sands history, and the history of the Strip. But it was not to be.

Adelson made a deal with the producers of *Con Air*, an action-adventure movie starring Nicolas Cage, to crash a plane into the casino. The film crew made the hotel look like opening day with new light bulbs and working slot machines.

The Sands Hotel thanks the public for "44 great years." Image courtesy of the Nevada State Museum, Las Vegas.

A two-day auction began on July 30, 1996, as the Sands was sold off bit by bit. Slot machines, blackjack tables, craps tables, roulette wheels, and more went on the auction block.

In August, the asbestos was removed to prepare for the demolition of the hotel. Don Payne, the former manager of the Las Vegas News Bureau, talked to Frank Wright at the Nevada State Museum, Las Vegas. Together they were able to save a number of historic items, including items from the historic bomb shelter that had been on the property, prior to the demolition.

On November 26, 1996, at 9:00 p.m., a huge crowd, that had gathered to watch, began the ten-second countdown. The main power switch was pulled and the marquee and tower lights went dark. The demolition began. It was all over rather quickly as the famed Martin Stern, Jr., tower came down to the ground while the crowd hooted and yelled.

In its place would be a new megaresort with 3,000 rooms, restaurants, shopping and luxury, the Venetian.

But it would never be the Sands.

The Venetian Hotel being built on the land where the Sands Hotel once stood. Image courtesy of the Nevada State Museum, Las Vegas.

9

THE ROYAL NEVADA
1955-1958

THE ILL-FATED HOTEL

The 1950s and Las Vegas are part of our collective memory. Too often though, the myth of those times takes precedence over the real history of that fabulous decade. The 1950s saw the Las Vegas Strip grow in size and in tourists but one of the stories that often gets lost in the myth-making is the story of the Royal Nevada, the eighth resort built on the Las Vegas Strip.

1955 was a busy, exciting year for the Strip. The Royal Nevada was one of three new hotels that would open throughout the year, and rumors abounded that the Strip was being over-built because many wondered how the Strip could sustain itself with so many hotels vying for tourists' attention. The well-known adage that if "you build it they will come" seemed to work for the other two hotels that opened that year, the Riviera and the Dunes, but the Royal Nevada was jinxed almost from the beginning.

Frank Fishman, a California hotel operator, began building his new resort, tentatively called "Nevada Royal" on December 1, 1953. The cost was pegged at $5 million, and the resort would feature an Olympic sized pool. Architect Paul Revere Williams, one of the most renowned African-American architects working in that era, was in charge of the design of the resort. Williams worked with John Replogie on the project. The entrance of the hotel was designed with a curvy canopy that provided shade in the summer to those arriving at the hotel and a large fountain-like sculpture of neon. (Alan Hess, *Viva Las Vegas: After-Hours Architecture*)

Though Frank Fishman owned the resort, he quickly ran into financial troubles and started looking around for buyers. The Nevada Tax Commission (predecessor to the Gaming Commission) announced that the majority partners, Frank Fishman, Sam "Game Boy" Miller, and Herbert "Pittsy" Manheim were "totally undesirable citizens for Nevada," and that they would not approve the casino's

The entrance to the Royal Nevada Hotel. Image courtesy of the Nevada State Museum, Las Vegas.

The Young Electric Sign Company (YESCO) has help delivering the roadside sign crown to the Royal Nevada Hotel. Image courtesy of the Nevada State Museum, Las Vegas.

application for a gaming license. Miller and Manheim were, according to the commission, well-known illegal gambling operators in Michigan and Florida. (David G. Schwartz, *The Long, Hot Summer of 1955*, Vegas Seven, August 6, 2015)

Before the resort even opened, Fishman sold his interests in the hotel to A. B. Moll, Sid Wyman, and Barnett Rosenthal. The gaming license was issued to a woman, Roberta May Simon, who owned a 10% interest in the hotel.

Above ground atomic testing had become a part of Southern Nevada living since the first test at the Nevada Test Site in 1951. Since then the resorts, especially the Sands, and the Las Vegas News Bureau, had sought ways to publicize the town and the bombs. On the night before the official opening, the Royal Nevada had a pre-opening party for the atomic soldiers at the Nevada Test Site soldiers, and they were bussed into town and given the run of the hotel and casino.

The Royal Nevada was billed as the Showplace of Showtown, USA. Befitting its royal name, a crown set atop the pylon beckoning all who entered. At the time of its opening, the Royal Nevada had the largest gift shop of any of the hotels and was managed by Bud Harris.

The hotel officially opened on April 19, 1955. It was located just north of the New Frontier on the west side of the Highway. Eddie Rio, a thirty-three-year show business veteran, was hired as the entertainment director. He announced

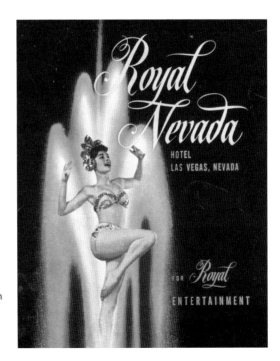

The Royal Nevada Showroom program cover. Image courtesy of the Nevada State Museum, Las Vegas.

that he was planning on bringing Broadway-style theater to Las Vegas. He hired musician Jerry Fielding to conduct the house orchestra.

In the showroom, called appropriately enough the Crown Room, Helen Traubel, a well-known opera star, with comedic assistance from Dave Barry, was showcased and the Dukes of Dixieland were headlining the Lounge. Many reporters were in town for the opening of both the Royal Nevada and the Riviera (which opened a day after the Royal Nevada). With the spotlight on two resort hotels opening, the media coverage favored the Riviera, which had the distinction of being the first high-rise on the Las Vegas Strip, topping nine stories.

As part of Eddie Rio's promise to up the theatrical value of Las Vegas shows, the Royal Nevada management showcased the Dancing Waters. The Waters had made their American debut at Radio City Music Hall in 1953 and had become an international sensation. (David G. Schwartz, *The Long, Hot Summer of 1955*)

The waters moved in rhythm with music thanks to a 48-foot mechanism that held 4,000 jets that forced 38 tons of water as high as 50 feet in the air. (David G. Schwartz, *The Long, Hot Summer of 1955*)

Everyone hoped it would become a Las Vegas sensation.

Sometime in the summer of 1955, a temporary lease on the resort was signed with Jake Kozloff, who had a number of interests in various hotels up and down the Strip.

Facts get a little fuzzy in trying to sort everything out, but by the fall of 1955, some say that Bill Miller, who had done so much to turn the Sahara into a nightclub paradise as their entertainment director, jumped ship and bought the Royal Nevada. On October 8, 1955, Bill Miller took ownership of the property. Later that month, it was announced that a group of Southwest businessmen had invested $1 million in Royal Nevada.

The entertainment at the Royal Nevada, even with Bill Miller at the helm, never reached the heights of other Strip hotels such as the Sahara, the Sands, or even the El Rancho Vegas or the New Frontier. Its headliners included Anna Maria Alberghetti and a host of second tier entertainers such as Marilyn Maxwell, Robert Alda, and Vivian Blaine.

The Royal Nevada was shuttered, briefly, on January 1, 1956, due to money owed, some say as much as $4,000 in back wages, to Culinary Union employees, which makes it very odd if Bill Miller owned the Royal Nevada. He had owned his own club, the Riviera—not to be confused with the Las Vegas hotel of the same name—back in New Jersey. He was an experienced hand at owning and running a nightclub. He had transformed the entertainment scene at the Sahara Hotel, ushering in the age of the lounge, by hiring Louis Prima and Keely Smith.

But close it did. According to local lawyer Ralph Denton, he received a late-night phone call about 11 p.m. from Joe McDonald, another lawyer who represented the owners of the Royal Nevada. According to Denton, the hotel was closing because they couldn't pay their licensing fee and they had to have it to remain operational in the new year. Needless to say, all the New Year's Day dinners, which had been pre-prepared so that they would only need re-heating, would go to waste. Instead of that happening, Denton and McDonald loaded up their station wagons and delivered turkey dinners to all their friends and all the charitable organizations in town, including the local hospitals. And there was still, Denton remembered sadly, enough left over food for the McDonald and Denton families to enjoy as well. (Personal interview with the author, 2005)

Jake Kozloff, who was part of the New Frontier Hotel ownership, announced in February that he had a lease on the place. Unfortunately for Kozloff, he could not turn a profit on the property.

In March of 1956, the Royal Nevada reopened, and by the summer, it had new owners. The Nevada Tax Board, forerunner of the Gaming Commission, deferred action on an application for a license by the new owners. One of those

Jake Kozloff was a familiar face on the Las Vegas Strip. Image courtesy of the Belknap Collection, Nevada State Museum, Las Vegas.

owners was T. W. "Rich" Richardson, owner of the Broadwater Beach Hotel in Biloxi, Mississippi. Bucky Harris, the owner of the famed North Shore Club in Lake Tahoe, became general manager.

But by 1958, the hotel was shuttered for good. Stan Irwin, of the Sahara, talked CBS into doing a live television show promoting the Sahara Hotel. It was to be filmed in Las Vegas but Stan didn't want to disrupt the customers at the Sahara, so he made arrangements for the interiors and entertainment segments to be filmed at the shuttered Royal Nevada.

The mid-1950s were a rough patch for the hotels on the Strip because it was the only time that the number of rooms exceeded the number of tourists. The Riviera and the Dunes would hang-on, thanks largely in part to the entertainment choices their seasoned entertainment directors made. Liberace became a staple at the Riviera, playing to sold-out crowds, and The Dunes brought in *Minksy's Burlesque* with topless dancers, which caused an uproar up and down the boulevard.

The Royal Nevada never did re-open. In 1959, the Stardust bought the property and it became the Stardust Auditorium with a giant neon *S* and *A* replacing the crown on the pylon. The garden-style motel rooms and the Olympic sized pool became part of the Stardust Hotel.

The rumpled crown from the pylon rests in the Neon Museum's Boneyard.

The Royal Nevada crown rests in the Neon Museum Boneyard. Image courtesy of Allen Sandquist.

10

THE RIVIERA
1955-2015

SEEING THE FUTURE

1955 was an interesting year for the Las Vegas Strip. Three resorts appeared in the glistening desert—the Royal Nevada and the Riviera opened within a day of one another and the Dunes would open a month later, but all three would struggle financially.

The Casa Blanca Hotel—as the Riviera was originally to be called—ran into problems before even the first spade of dirt had been turned. The Nevada Tax Commission—the precursor to the Nevada Gaming Commission—in researching the original licensee applicants, discovered that one of them had deep ties to Meyer Lansky. The red flags went up and the word went out to find a new set of partners. (Jeff Burbank, *Online Nevada*)

While construction started, new partners were found and the Nevada Tax Commission issued licenses to David, Lou and Meyer Gensburg, Jack Goldman, RH Bailey, Murray Saul, Harpo Marx, and Gummo Marx.

The Riviera continued to create a stir before her doors ever opened because the hotel was a visual and architectural departure from the low-rise, two-story garden-style motel rooms that had been popular since the early days of the 1940s. The Riviera was going vertical, nine stories into the air, the first high-rise on the famed boulevard, and with a price tag of $10 million. The hotel would have 291 rooms. According to architecture historian Alan Hess, there was even some question around town as to whether the desert soil would even support such a structure.

The architectural firm of Roy France and Son was hired to design the innovative hotel. France envisioned utilizing design elements of the streamlined Sands Hotel that had been built in 1939 down in Miami, Florida. Working with the firm was local architect, J. Maher Weller. The construction was done by Taylor Construction Company, who would build three other resorts over the years, including the Tropicana, the International, and the original MGM Grand Hotel.

Model of the Riviera Hotel. Image courtesy of UNLV's Special Collections.

The first high-rise hotel and casino is coming. Image courtesy of UNLV's Special Collections.

The *porte cochere* at the Riviera Hotel. Image courtesy of the Nevada State Museum, Las Vegas.

A block with banks of horizontal strip windows marked the center of the tower, and wrap-around windows delineating the corners were added. The contrasting elevator tower, with decorative gold buttons, definitely conjured up images of South Beach Miami instead of the Southwest. The various floors were named after French resort cities such as Cannes, Monaco, and Nice. The ninth-floor penthouse suites housed a state-of-the-art health club.

The pylon sign "skewered the thin *porte-cochere* like a toothpick through a cheese canapé," according to Alan Hess. There was a second V-shaped marquee sign at the roadside entrance. (Alan Hess, *Viva Las Vegas: After-Hours Architecture*)

The interiors recalled the famed Miami Beach hotel, the Fountainbleau. The lobby and front desk area featured Italian marble and corrugated copper fixtures. The Starlight Lounge, just off the lobby, had a 150-foot free-form stage bar. The lighting fixtures were brass in a starburst design against a teal-blue sky canopy, mimicking a moonlit night.

The Hickory Room Restaurant was designed in Western style, paneled throughout in wormwood. Open hickory fires and a huge rotisserie were in view of the diners. The Coffee Shop—which later became Cafe Noir—was actually two restaurants with one section designed for swimmers. There was a poolside-dining terrace called Le Bistro, which was shaded, in part, by numerous redwood trees imported from California.

The hotel's construction went down to the wire with the resort opening while the paint was still drying. Over half of the musicians for the orchestra came from Los Angeles, because there weren't enough players in town.

The Riviera opened its doors on April 20, 1955, and by most accounts, it was a lavish affair. Liberace and his brother, George, were the headliners. Actress Joan Crawford was the official hostess, and she reportedly received $10,000 for four days of greeting guests. Other perks included a free room and meals.

The hiring of Liberace seriously upped the ante on what it cost to put on a show in Las Vegas. Liberace was receiving a record-breaking $50,000 a week, but just a few years previously, he had been playing the New Frontier for $750 a week.

At the Riviera, a thirty-two-piece orchestra conducted by his brother, George, accompanied him. George often told the story of how he and Lee had met Jack Goldman—one of the original owners of the Riviera—on a plane trip to Florida. Goldman explained that he was building the tallest resort in Las Vegas and needed a headliner. Having heard many a visionary, Liberace explained that they were very loyal to the Frontier. Goldman then made his lavish offer. The Liberace brothers left the New Frontier, and international designer Christan Dior designed

Liberace surrounded by friends and guests. Image courtesy of the Nevada State Museum, Las Vegas.

Liberace's dazzling white tuxedo that he wore on his opening night on the stage of the Clover Room, the showroom where Liberace held court. It had seating for 532 for the dinner show and 700 for the late show. With six separate elevations and a 40 x 80 foot stage, it was the first to use four revolving turntables. At 10,000 square feet it was the largest showroom on the Strip and would be utilized to the max by the Riviera's top headliner, Liberace. The room was draped in platinum gray velour with a jet-black ceiling illuminated by starlit constellations.

The Treniers opened the Starlite Lounge. The Treniers were already an established lounge act in Las Vegas, having played the various hotels including the El Rancho Vegas and the Hotel Last Frontier. With their rollicking rock and roll sound and good-natured humor, the group kept the lounge jumping until the early hours of the morning.

The Riviera seemed to open at the right time and coincided with the Desert Inn's Tournament of Champions, another atomic test detonation at the Nevada Test Site, and a light heavyweight boxing match between champion Archie Moore and contender Nino Valdez. Journalists and reporters from around the world covered the opening, but it wasn't enough to keep the hotel from running in the red. The Miami-based operators were unaccustomed to gambling, and the hotel slid towards bankruptcy. The Gensburg brothers began quickly looking for new operators to run the hotel.

They quickly hired Gus Greenbaum, Ben Goffstein, Harry S. Goldman, Ross Miller (father of future governor, Bob Miller), Davey Berman, Jess Goldman, Charles Harrison, and Frank, Fred and Elias Atol to take over the sinking resort and fix the problems. (Jeff Burbank, *Online Nevada*)

Greenbaum and Berman had been associated with the fabulous Flamingo and had been part of the group that took control of that hotel in the wake of Bugsy Siegel's murder in Beverly Hills.

Greenbaum had retired to Scottsdale but his "bosses" in Chicago wanted him to return to Las Vegas and work his magic once again. According to Steve Fischer, Greenbaum was told "Vegas is where you belong." (Steve Fischer, *When the Mob Ran Vegas*)

Greenbaum fought the decision to move back to Las Vegas. After his sister-in-law was found murdered in her bed, Greenbaum and his wife, Bess, packed the car and returned to Las Vegas.

The new operators attracted some unwanted attention. By June, the Nevada Tax Commission wanted a complete probe of the hotel.

On July 28, Greenbaum applied to the Nevada Tax Commission to become the managing director of the Riviera. In his application, Greenbaum stated that he had a previous good reputation with the Flamingo, and he would be hiring some of those same people to join him at the Riviera. Greenbaum also stated that he and his group had loaned the Riviera $500,000 to continue operating. (Jeff Burbank, *Online Nevada*)

On Sept. 28, the Tax Commission agreed to lease the casino at the Riviera to Greenbaum and his partners. The Commission noted that the staggering debt of the hotel and the pressure of creditors were the main factors in their decision. Out of the fourteen applicants, only eight were approved. Greenbaum, Goffstein, and Berman were back in business.

The new operators began to right the listing ship that had been the Riviera. They cleaned house, stopped the pilfering and soon the hotel was making a profit.

Liberace was still the top headliner. Other top acts that played "The Riv" in the 1950s include Orson Welles and his magic act. When questioned by local newspaper columnist, Forrest Duke, if his act was a secret, Welles replied in his rich baritone, "It isn't a secret, but it's a mystery to me." (Mike Weatherford, *Cult Vegas*)

Ken Murray's *Blackouts* with Marie Wilson, Dinah Shore, and George White's *Scandals* were some of the others to play the Riviera. Elvis Presley, performing at the New Frontier, caught Liberace's act one evening. Liberace invited Elvis on stage and the two traded places, Liberace on guitar and Elvis at Lee's grand piano.

The Nite of Stars, a yearly fundraiser for St. Jude's Ranch for Children, a cause that was important to comedian Danny Thomas, was held at the Riviera in 1958.

Liberace and Elvis swap personas onstage at the Riviera. Image courtesy of UNLV's Special Collections.

Bob Hope, who, surprisingly, never headlined in Las Vegas, Lucille Ball, and other top acts performed from the stage of the Clover Room to an overflow crowd that had paid $100 a person to attend.

While the Riviera was finally financial stable, Gus Greenbaum's life was spinning out of control. According to Steve Fischer, Greenbaum's Chicago "friends" were becoming increasingly unhappy with his out-of-control lifestyle. Riviera investor—and Chicago mobster—Marshall Caifano, accused Greenbaum of taking more than his share of Riviera profits. (Jeff Burbank, *Online Nevada*)

Adding to the spiral, Greenbaum's friend, gangster, and union thug, Willie Bioff, was killed when he was blown up along with his car outside a home in Phoenix. Greenbaum's partner, Davey Berman, took ill and the prognosis was cancer. Berman died a short while later. Bess Greenbaum, never liking the Las Vegas lifestyle of her husband, returned to Phoenix in the fall of 1958.

Greenbaum, drinking too much and rumored to have a heroin problem, decided to spend the Thanksgiving holiday that year with his family in Phoenix. On the morning of Dec. 3, the housekeeper found Mr. and Mrs. Gus Greenbaum dead. Bess Greenbaum's body was found in the living room. Greenbaum's body was found in the bedroom. Their throats had been slashed. Not surprisingly, the murderer was never found. (Steve Fischer, *When the Mob Ran Vegas*)

A memorial service was held in Las Vegas for the Greenbaums at Temple Beth Shalom on Dec. 5, 1958. Rabbi Bernard Cohen and Cantor Herman Kinnory presided over the service. In the audience were local dignitaries, journalists, and top executives from the Riviera. The Phoenix coroner ruled that the deaths were murder. Vice-president of the Riviera, Ben Goffstein, announced a $25,000 reward for information leading to the capture of the killer(s). There were rumors flying around about the reason for the Greenbaum killings, but an investigator for the Nevada Tax Commission found no link between Nevada gambling and the deaths.

Ben Goffstein was elevated to President of the Riviera, given a watch for his excellent service to the hotel, and promptly checked into a local hospital where he was diagnosed with physical exhaustion and told to take it easy. By October, the remodeling was kicked up a notch, and it was announced that the hotel would undergo a $3.5 million expansion, which would add 114 rooms to the resort, and would bring the total visitor spaces to 415 guest rooms. A Sky Room was planned for the tenth floor that would feature dusk-to-dawn dancing.

By 1959, the Riviera was starting to remodel some of its interiors. The Starlight Lounge makeover further separated it from the gambling areas while Bernard of Hollywood, one of the premiere portrait artists in the greater Los Angeles area, opened a studio in the hotel.

As the 1960s dawned, the Riviera was preparing to make the most of its assets.

The lobby of the Riviera Hotel. Image courtesy of the Nevada State Museum, Las Vegas.

Exterior of the Riviera with its original marquee. Liberace is in the Clover Room and the Treniers are in the Starlite Lounge. Image courtesy of As We Knew It: Classic Las Vegas Collection.

A TORNADO NAMED SHECKY

As the 1960s began, the Riviera Hotel was undergoing a multi-million dollar expansion while still trying to get past the death of Gus Greenbaum. On July 7, the Nevada Tax Commission approved the sale of 15% of the hotel's stock in the Greenbaum estate be sold back to the hotel for $120,000. The estate still retained a 17% interest in the hotel.

Two weeks later, Ben Goffstein informed the Tax Commission that unless there was a major infusion of cash into the hotel, they would have to shut down. Goffstein was hoping that the Commission would grant permission for owners of the Desert Inn and the Stardust to step in and help the financially struggling resort. According to Goffstein, the debt of the hotel far exceeded the operating money on hand with major payments and payroll that still had to be paid. Goffstein requested that Wilbur Clark, Allen Roen, Moe Dalitz, and the other Desert Inn/Stardust licensees be approved to step in. The other licensees would put $760,000 into the operation budget of the hotel and keep it from defaulting on its loans and its payroll. Goffstein stressed that the Riv was not bankrupt, just cash poor. (Jeff Burbank, *Online Nevada*)

Shecky Greene onstage.
Image courtesy of
Bo Boisvert.

The Commissioners listened to Goffstein's proposal. In addition to the money that the licensees were putting up already, they would guarantee an additional $250,000 loan from the First National Bank of Nevada. This infusion of funds would help to keep the resort open while the Tax Commission debated what to do next. The Commission, to their credit, did not want to be a rubber stamp this time around. They agreed to the money arrangement and would hand down a final decision regarding the property later in the summer.

In the back of everyone's mind seemed to be the financial and economic implications if the resort were to be closed. Such a high-profile closure would send a signal not only throughout the state but internationally as well. The Royal Nevada had closed in 1955 amid concerns that the famed boulevard was overbuilt. Since then, three more hotels—the Dunes, the Stardust, and the Hacienda—had opened, and the remodeling the older hotels were undertaking sent a message that Las Vegas was the place to vacation. A hit to the economy of the Strip was something no one wanted to face.

While the Tax Commission debated what to do, the Riviera stayed open. By the fall, the Commission approved Charles Harrison's application for 2% interest in the resort. But, the members of the Commission demanded clarification on the infiltration of the resort by key personnel of the Desert Inn. The Desert Inn had been denied its offer to purchase the Riviera by the Commission, but now the Commission discovered that they were assuming management of the Riviera in addition to helping out financially. The Desert Inn licensees claimed that they were only hiring the best personnel for the job.

On Nov. 25, Attorney General Roger Foley ruled in favor of the Tax Commission and said they had the power to halt the "infiltration of key personnel," however, certain procedures had to be followed. In addition, the Riviera would have the opportunity to seek judicial review. If the higher court ruled in favor of the Tax Commission, then the Commission could take disciplinary action on the conditions not met.

The matter continued, and the Riviera stayed open.

Due to all the problems with the Tax Commission and the financial problems with the hotel, the $3.5 million expansion that had been planned in 1959 didn't get rolling until 1962. The expansion called for eleven more stories to be built, which would add an additional 120 lanai rooms overlooking the patio and pool area.

One of the happier events to occur late that year was the name change of the showroom. The Clover Room was renamed the Versailles Room and showcased a great line-up of talent including Louis Armstrong, Betty Grable, Tony Bennett, George Burns, the Andrew Sisters, and Sid Caesar. The dressing rooms in the Versailles Room were to be enlarged and the casino and lobby were to be redecorated.

Moe Dalitz. Image courtesy of UNLV's
Special Collections.

Despite all the financial problems, the hotel was slowly righting itself one more time. Many old-timers credit a powerhouse lounge comedian for keeping the crowds coming to the Riviera. That comedian just happened to be Shecky Greene.

"Shecky Greene was almost single-handedly responsible for keeping the hotel in business," recalled Riviera publicist Tony Zoppi. "He consistently brought the high rollers to his show and to the hotel." (*Las Vegas Sun Sunday Magazine*, July 1, 1979)

Greene had been playing Las Vegas since the 1950s. In fact, he was part of the billing when a young Elvis Presley played the Hotel Last Frontier. Like Liberace, Greene had bolted from the Frontier when the Riviera offered more money. Greene would become a staple at the Riviera before leaving in the 1970s for the original MGM Grand Hotel.

By 1963, Ben Goffstein had been running the hotel for seven years. He was tired. He also had his eye on piece of property on Fremont Street, away from the nightlife of the Strip. He dreamed of a hotel/casino named after the most important women in his life, his wife and daughters, whom he called his "4 Queens." In February, he resigned to make that dream a reality.

Riviera marquee publicizing Liberace and extra-added attraction Barbra Streisand in her Las Vegas debut. Image courtesy of As We Knew It: Classic Las Vegas Collection.

That year, a young, up-and-coming singer from New York, Barbra Streisand, made her Las Vegas debut as the opening act for Liberace.

A reviewer for the *Hollywood Reporter* wrote, "Singer Barbra Streisand was a sharp contrast to [Liberace]. Her make-up made her look like something that just climbed off a broom, but when she sang, it was like the wailing of a banshee bouncing up and down on marionette strings. It isn't until she does three or four songs that her voice is even noticed as being very pleasant. Her outrageous grooming almost nullifies her talent." (*The Barbra Streisand Archives*)

Six years later, in 1969, she would return as headliner and open the International Hotel.

In November of that year, the Riviera joined the other resorts on the Strip in dimming their lights in the wake of the assassination of President Kennedy and his funeral on Nov. 25.

By 1965, Hotel Riviera Inc. bought out the interests of the Gensbro Company, thus becoming the sole owner of the property. Harvey Silbert, Harry S. Goldman, and Broadway producer David Merrick retained their interests in the hotel. Ross Miller stayed on as Chairman of the Board, Jess Goodman remained as president and Charles Harrison continued as executive vice-president.

David Merrick brought *Hello, Dolly!*, starring actress-singer Betty Grable, to the Riviera. The Broadway musical directed by Gower Champion proved to be a huge hit. After Grable finished her stint as Dolly Levi, Dorothy Lamour and then Ginger Rogers took her place.

Another expansion began in 1968 with the announcement of a south wing that would hold 770 rooms, suites, and a convention center. The cost was $5 million for the twelve-story tower.

Offices for four major airlines leased space on the ground floor, and the shopping promenade was updated as well. Keeping with the French theme, the doormen wore uniforms reminiscent of the French Foreign Legion. The main floor included a 13,000-square-foot convention hall. Upstairs on the second floor was the Normandy Room with an additional 2,800 square feet of convention facilities, including seating for 400.

In late 1968, Harvey Silbert, Daniel Merrick, and Jerry Mack—of the fabled Bank of Las Vegas/Valley Bank—who had become a stock holder through a trust account, partnered with Ed Torres to buy out the rest of the stock holders, including Harrison, Miller, and Goodman. Speculation was rampant that Parvin-Dohrmann, which both Silbert and Torres were officers of, would buy the hotel. Instead, Torres put in $240,000 by purchasing 32% of its stock and becoming the major stockholder. Torres was named president, a position he held until he stepped down in 1978.

Shecky Greene and Ed Torres did not get along. The animosity between the two was so intense that Greene told staffers to keep Torres out of the lounge when he was on stage. One night, Greene got the news just before he went onstage that they were relocating the lounge and turning the current lounge into a Keno Parlor. Greene took the stage with a pickaxe in hand and spent his show chopping the stage into souvenirs and passing them out to the audience. The next day, Ed Torres, reportedly unaware of what Greene had done the night before, called to say that they were putting the construction plans on hold. Greene's exploits at the hotel are legendary, and he was fired numerous times, but the Riviera could not afford for him to stay fired. As often as they would fire him, they would hire him back.

Greene was one of the biggest draws in town. His unpredictability along with his stream of consciousness kept the audience on their toes. They never knew what mood he would be in or what routines he would have in his act. His improvisational style had many thinking he just made up his routines as he went along. The Riv was paying him $20,000 a week with a twenty-six-week guarantee. He was the late-night anchor in the lounge, and every night it was usually standing-room only. (Mike Weatherford, *Cult Vegas*)

But Greene was also a heavy drinker and a heavy gambler. The hotel had cut off his credit in an effort to help stem his gambling losses. One night after his

The always-unpredictable Shecky Greene. Image courtesy of Bo Boisvert.

act, he was headed to the Hacienda—the only place on the Strip that would still extend him credit. He was speeding down Las Vegas Blvd. South when he lost control of his Cadillac, struck a pole in front of Caesars Palace, flipped the car twice, hit the low pony wall, and landed in the fountain. By the time the police got there, he was said to have quipped, "No spray wax" before they handcuffed him and hauled him off to jail. Entertainer and friend, Sonny King, made his bail. In reality, what Greene actually said was, "I guess I'm arrested." Once he was free on bail, he and Buddy Hackett came up with the "no spray wax" line and both would tell the tale for years using that line. (Mike Weatherford, *Cult Vegas*)

As the 1960s came to a close, Dean Martin's long-running contract with the Sands came to an end. He moved over to the Riviera. He became a 10% owner and the hotel opened Dino's Den, a cozy lounge-type room, for him.

Dean Martin opened at the Riviera in June of 1969. With his weekly television show featuring the Gold Diggers and his hit movies such as *Five Card Stud*, he was a household name. Frank Sinatra did not attend opening night, but he was in the audience the next night.

The Riviera in the 1970s with the Ben Chapman designed roadside sign. Image courtesy of Joel Rosales, Lost & Found Vegas.

NOT ENOUGH LIVES

On Sept. 12, 1970 the Riviera hosted a historical event, the Friar's Club Roast in honor of comedian, Joe E. Lewis. It was, even by Las Vegas standards, a bawdy, blue-aired, memorable night. Dean Martin was the host, and General George Jessel was the emcee. Guests included: Marty Allen, Jack Benny, George Burns, Jimmy Durante, Buddy Hackett, Fat Jack E. Leonard, Tony Martin, the Lemon Drop Kid, "Swifty" Morgan, Jan Murray, famed restaurateur Toots Shor, Phil Silvers, Ed Sullivan, Louis Armstrong, Pearl Bailey, Telly Savalas, and a bevy of local and state dignitaries, including Governor Paul Laxalt, hoteliers Nate Jacobson and Jay Sarno, and a packed house of Hollywood's and Broadway's finest.

Joe E. Lewis was a vaudeville legend. Sinatra had portrayed him in the film *The Joker is Wild*. He had started his career on the South Side of Chicago where he had a run-in with Al Capone's gang. The run-in had left him almost dead, with his vocal chords cut. Though Capone liked Lewis, he would not move against one of his own. Instead, he provided Lewis with the necessary money to recover both physically and professionally. Lewis was one of the first to realize the potential of performing in Las Vegas. Sinatra, a long-time fan, was usually in the audience for Lewis' shows when he was in Las Vegas and that insured that his friends and entourage were there as well.

Lewis was also an inveterate gambler known to lose hundreds of dollars at a time at the tables. By 1970, Lewis had suffered a debilitating stroke and was, according to writer Mike Weatherford, a ghost of his former self.

The Riviera's modern *porte cochere* combined neon and flicker bulbs for a stunning effect. Image courtesy of Joel Rosales, Lost & Found Vegas.

Joe E. Lewis, according to lounge pioneer Freddie Bell, did not drink during the day. "He played gin. But he would make up for it at night. I tried to drink like him, and it damn near killed me." Image courtesy of As We Knew It: Classic Las Vegas Collection.

Dean Martin introduced Lewis that evening as, "The greatest saloon comic ever. He taught me how to drink, and I am beholden to him for that," to which Lewis quipped, "If I thought you were going to eulogize me, I would have done the decent thing and died first."

Sinatra was supposed to co-host the event but due to a spate of bad press over his run-in with Sanford Waterman at Caesars, he opted to keep the focus on Lewis and stayed away.

By the time it came for Lewis to address the 1,300 crowd of friends and family, there was not a dry eye in the house, according to local columnist Forrest Duke. "He tried to complete his takeoff on (the song), 'My Way' but not many of the funny lines—'I know I drank a lot, threw up on every highway/I was a souse, but not a louse, I did it my way'—were barely audible to the guests but when he proclaimed 'It's Post Time!' the crowd went wild and gave him a standing ovation." (Mike Weatherford, *Cult Vegas*)

Afterwards, Lewis returned to New York City, went into diabetic coma, and died within days.

By 1972, Dean Martin was unhappy with his partners at the Riviera. They were all embroiled in a contract dispute, and Martin was locked out of his usual suite. Martin had suggested he would perform one show a night which would have set a precedent in a town where two shows a night were mandatory. One official noted that since Martin had moved from the Sands to the Riviera, there had been an increase in high rollers at the Riviera. Martin finally tired of the fighting and received a better offer. He sold his interest in the Riviera and finished out his contract.

In 1972, Conrad Hilton contemplated buying the property but upon surveying it and not seeing much room for expansion, he decided to keep looking.

Meshulam Riklis, who would become better known as the husband of Hollywood starlet Pia Zadora, was, in 1973, the majority stockholder of American International Travel Services (AITS). He bought the Riviera for $56 million. AITS had been losing money since 1960 and speculation was rampant about how Riklis planned to finance the buy. In 1972, AITS had recorded a loss of $4.11 a share, and AITS had been forced to sell the Hawaiian Regent Hotel, which was used for the company's Hawaiian package tours. Riklis used loans from the Nevada Employees Retirement System to shore up the hotel. (Jeff Burbank, *Online Nevada*)

Shecky Greene, too, wanted out of his contract. At the heart of Greene's dispute was the fact that the hotel owed him money. Caesars Palace was rumored to want Greene. He could perform once a night at Caesars. Don Rickles was rumored to want out of his contract as well.

In July, the hotel released Dean Martin from his contract, so that he could formally sign with Kirk Kerkorian to play the original MGM Grand Hotel once it was completed.

The Ben Chapman
designed roadside sign
for the Riviera Hotel.
Image courtesy of As We
Knew It: Classic Las Vegas
Collection.

By 1975, the Riviera added a seventeen-story tower called the Monte Carlo. The tower cost $20 million and included 300 rooms, sixty suites, and an elaborate penthouse. The hotel also had a new sign designed by Ben Chapman.

In 1977, they added the San Remo tower with an additional 200 rooms. The tower was located on the south side of the resort. They also opened the Ristorante Italiano, a gourmet Italian eatery that seated 100.

Riklis' wife, Pia Zadora, made her Las Vegas debut at the hotel performing in the Versailles Room as the opening act for comedian Bob Newhart. Zadora would make a name for herself a few years later as "Best New Star of the Year," a designation bestowed by the Hollywood Foreign Press. She was given a Golden Globe award for basically removing her clothes in the film, *Butterfly*. Rumors flew that Riklis had enticed the Hollywood Foreign Press with lavish junkets to Las Vegas to secure their votes for his wife.

By 1984, the hotel had run out of luck again and filed Chapter 11 bank-ruptcy. Arthur Waltzman, a CPA, was brought in to help right the listing hotel. Waltzman, who understood tourists, began to target not only the high rollers but the middle-class tourist as well. He marketed the hotel as a fun place to gamble and to hang out. By 1985, the Riviera was back.

Riviera marquee publicizing "All-New, King of Cool" *Splash!* Image courtesy of As We Knew It: Classic Las Vegas Collection.

In 1985, *Splash!*, starring impressionist Frank Gorshin, debuted in the Versailles Room. This aquacade of music and dance, according to the local critics of the day, took place in and around a 20,000-gallon aquarium and featured numerous performers and specialty acts. The show racked up all kinds of awards.

In the Mardi Gras Showroom, a young impersonator named Frank Marino who specialized in female performers, opened as part of a new show called *An Evening at La Cage*. Marino was barely twenty years old. *Boylesque*, starring female impersonator Kenny Kerr, was a smash hit at the Silver Slipper and the Riviera saw the chance to cash in on not only that success, but the Broadway musical *La Cage aux Folles*, which was taking New York by storm.

Budd Friedman, who owned The Improv—with clubs in both New York and Los Angeles—signed a partnership deal with the Rivera to put one of his clubs in the hotel. The Riviera also opened another show, *Crazy Girls*, which became famous for its provocative billboard and taxi ads.

In 1988, the Riviera was successful enough to add the twenty-four-story Monaco Tower to its property. The $28 million tower nearly doubled the resort's rooms to 2,100. But the Las Vegas Strip was changing. The automobile culture, which the Strip had catered to from the beginning, was giving way. Steve Wynn was opening a new hotel, The Mirage, which would have a profound effect on the Strip and up the ante for years to come.

In these changing times of the Strip, the Riviera sought to hang on to its market. In 1990, they expanded the casino out to the property line. It brought the total square footage to 125,000, making it one of the largest casinos around. They offered slots, video poker and other video gambling, table games, poker, Keno, bingo and a complete sports book, but it was not enough.

Architect Nikita Zukov incorporated advertising signs and neon into what Alan Hess calls " a whip-curve facade with refractive glass". Marge Williams, one of the few female neon designers, designed the neon embellishments. (Alan Hess, *Viva Las Vegas: After-Hours Architecture*)

The hotel approached Burger King about opening a franchise on the property and Burger King agreed. Fast food had finally come to the Las Vegas Strip.

Frank Sinatra performed at the resort on New Year's Eve, 1990. He played to over 2,000 guests in the Superstar Theater. The hotel had to renovate one of its suites to Sinatra's specifications for the duration of his stay. Sinatra returned in 1991 for a four-day engagement.

Critics were basically mum on the fact that Sinatra was performing at a hotel that had a giant Burger King sign out front. Considering where they had all started from in the 1950s, this had to have seemed odd to more than just a few.

The neon and refractive glass exterior of the Riviera Hotel. Image courtesy of Joel Rosales, Lost & Found Vegas.

During the 1990s, the hotel was back in Chapter 11 bankruptcy, but owners managed to right the listing ship once more, even though the hotel seemed to be closing in on its nine lives. The hotel began to concentrate on the adult-oriented market at a time when Las Vegas was trying to become a family vacation destination. The adult marketing worked.

In a short amount of time, Frank Marino had gone from one of the female impersonators in *La Cage* to its main star. His impersonation of Joan Rivers kept the showroom crowded every night.

In 1994, *Splash!* underwent a $5 million renovation. One million was spent on renovating the Versailles Room. When the show re-opened, raincoats were offered to people who had certain seats. This new production had the feel of a submarine and there were few reminders of the previous show. There were more than 100 fountains, screens, and waterfalls, and a 100-foot U-shaped bridge that was equipped with sound and laser technology. An ice rink was built into the center of the stage. There were smoke and pyrotechnic effects. It took a year to build the show and the cost in costumes was rumored to be $80,000. One of the segments included the Globe of Death, which included a motorcycle with a Teflon coating, so that the motorcycle didn't stick to the ice.

Crazy Girls was still going strong, though county officials were getting complaints about the risqué billboards and taxicab advertisements. The hotel won

The terrazzo entrance to the Riviera Hotel. Image courtesy of Joel Rosales, Lost & Found Vegas.

the popularity contest in the media and had a bronze statue of the famous advertisement installed in front of the hotel.

Rubbing the female backsides for good luck became a tradition.

Hollywood came calling in 1994. Acclaimed director Martin Scorsese wanted to film his new movie *Casino* in Las Vegas. Loosely based on real-life events that had occurred on the Strip in the late 1970s and early 1980s, the movie was the story of Frank "Lefty" Rosenthal and Tony "The Ant" Spilotro. Based on the best-selling book by Nick Pelligi, Scorsese needed a hotel that still had that 1970s vibe.

The Riviera fit the bill. Management limited Scorsese to only filming interiors after hours (basically 10:00 p.m. to 6:00 a.m.) so as not to interfere with their customers and their penchant for privacy. Scorsese brought his cast, including Robert DeNiro, Joe Pesci, Sharon Stone, James Woods, and Don Rickles, along with his crew, to film all night. The film employed 246 local actors and several thousand extras. The movie wrapped production and was released to theaters in 1995. The film became a box-office success with an Academy Award nomination for Sharon Stone as Robert DeNiro's wife, Ginger.

With the demolition of the Dunes Hotel in the early 1990s to make room for the Bellagio, the Riviera became the last lady of 1955 still standing. Of the three

Liberace celebrates at the opening of the Riviera. Image courtesy of As We Knew It: Classic Las Vegas Collection.

hotels that had opened in 1955, the Royal Nevada had folded within a short time of opening, and the Dunes was destroyed amid a party atmosphere. The Riviera, however, was still open for business.

As the 1990s gave way to the twenty-first Century, the Riviera continued to hang on. It was one of the bastions of classic Las Vegas. Of the original hotels on the Strip, it was the one where you could chart the progression of the hotel through its architecture. Its pool still sported the mosaic tile and original logo. Standing poolside and looking around, you could see the original tower and each addition. Its shopping mezzanine still held ghosts of fashionable shops long gone.

On April 20, 2005, the Riviera celebrated its fiftieth anniversary with a four-day party, but progress was gaining the upper hand.

In the winter of 2015, the Las Vegas Convention and Visitors Authority announced that they had bought the Riviera. The current Las Vegas Convention Center needed to expand and the Convention Authority announced that the Riviera would close in the summer. The Riviera officially closed on May 4, 2015. Like the other hotels, its contents were auctioned off. In the winter of 2016, the hotel was prepped for demolition. Demolition of the hotel was set for June 14, 2016.

The hotel that had defied so much bad luck for so long finally ran out of lives.

11

THE DUNES
1955-1973

A MIRACLE IN THE DESERT

As we have seen, three hotels opened in the spring of 1955: The Royal Nevada, the Riviera, and the Dunes, but all three struggled to stay afloat that year. The Dunes was the tenth hotel and casino to open on what was quickly becoming known far and wide as the Fabulous Las Vegas Strip.

But, we are getting ahead of our story.

In the winter of 1954, it was announced that plans were moving forward on the building of a new hotel to be called the Dunes, and the cost was estimated at $5 million. Three major investors topped the list: Joseph Sullivan—a restaurateur from Providence, Rhode Island; Alfred Gottsman—a former theater magnet from Coral Gables, Florida; and Bob Rice, who had made his fortune as a costume jeweler in Beverly Hills. They all lacked one important addition to their investment resumes: none of these three major investors had gaming experience.

It was later believed that the funds that Sullivan had invested actually came from Ray Patriarca, the head of a Rhode Island crime family, in return for reaping the under-the-table profits that would be made from his undisclosed participation.

Before the hotel even opened, the owners announced plans to expand the property by constructing another 500 rooms and by adding a series of winter homes and a shopping complex.

The Dunes opened on May 23, 1955. It was located cater-corner across the highway from the Flamingo Hotel and at the time was the furthest hotel out on the south end of the highway. The Dunes had a *porte cochere* that was both modern and nomadic in style to impress the patrons and lure in the heavy gamblers.

Built in the low-rise tradition of many of the other hotels, the Dunes had a 35-foot tall, fiberglass Sultan, which was designed by YESCO. The colorful Sultan sported a flying cape with a plumed turban, and was a formidable figure as he stood astride the main entrance. The turban of the sultan included a sparkling

Image of the original Dunes Hotel, courtesy of the Nevada State Museum, Las Vegas.

The Dunes Sultan strides over the entrance to the hotel. Image courtesy of the Nevada State Museum, Las Vegas.

diamond that was actually a car headlight that had been gem-cut. He quickly joined the Pioneer Club's "Vegas Vic" as a glitzy roadside attraction.

The hotel had 200 rooms and a 90-foot pool created by architect Robert Dorr, Jr., of Hollywood, working with the architectural engineer John Replogle. A fountain with three sculpted sea horses rose from the center. There was a 150-foot long lagoon or reflecting pool surrounded by lilies, two fountains and a weeping willow. (Alan Hess, *Viva Las Vegas: After-Hours Architecture*) The construction of the hotel itself was completed by McNeil Construction Company of Los Angeles.

Opening in the stylish Arabian Room, whose proscenium stage was designed for Broadway shows, was MGM actress-dancer, Vera-Ellen. Choreographed by the show's director Robert Nesbitt, *The Magic Carpet Revue: New York-Paris Paradise* was the first Broadway-style revue to play Las Vegas. The stage's dimensions were 65 x 35 and included a revolving stage, a floating stage, as well as a remote-controlled lighting system that was said to rival the one used at Radio City Music Hall.

Unfortunately, by summer the hotel was in financial trouble, as tourism had not kept pace with the number of hotels opening and for the first time, there were more hotel rooms than guests. The Dunes had only opened with 200 units, which clearly was not enough space to accommodate the number of paying customers to secure overhead for the running of the hotel. Also adding to the problem was a finite number of high rollers and more hotels vying for their limited business.

The Sands Hotel was the most successful hotel on the Strip at the time, and the Dunes' management made a call for help. Jake Freedman listened to the pitch and soon thereafter, the Sands Hotel agreed to run the Dunes.

Jake Freedman appeared before the Nevada Tax Commission, stating that if the move was approved, Ed Levinson would be in charge of the casino, Carl Cohen would be in an advisory position, and Jack Entratter would be the entertainment director for both. The Nevada Tax Commission agreed to the arrangement. The management of the Sands put $600,000 in an escrow account to pay off the current owners' obligations. In addition, they put up $350,000 to subsidize the casino.

Charlie Tanner, Chuck Bennett, and Ed Levinson split their time between the two resorts. They tried to drum up publicity for the hotel by offering comps to Sands customers who would be willing to try the Dunes. Jack Entratter asked Frank Sinatra to play the Dunes. An all out publicity junket was planned. Sinatra, dressed like a character of the story *A Thousand and One Arabian Nights*, rode in on a camel.

Entratter booked Maurice Chevalier, Cab Calloway, and Sophie Tucker as well. Still, it wasn't enough.

Frank Sinatra and Entertainment Director Jack Entratter at the Dunes Hotel after the Sands took over management. Image courtesy of UNLV's Special Collections.

"The Sands kept pouring money into the Dunes without any luck and finally threw in the towel," Chuck Bennett recounted to writer George Stamos in a 1979 interview. (*Las Vegas Sun Sunday Magazine*, July 15, 1979)

Finally, the management realized that the Dunes was a money pit and a financial drain on their main concern, the Sands. They closed the casino and operated the hotel as a motel.

Jake Gottlieb, who owned Western Transportation out of Chicago, became interested in the property. Gottlieb received investment help from the Teamsters Union Pension Fund, which was handled by the notorious James "Jimmy" Hoffa. Gottlieb purchased the property. But Gottlieb, like so many others, didn't have any experience running a casino. He began looking for someone with imagination and daring and got lucky when he stumbled upon Major Arteburn Riddle, who also owned a shipping company out of Chicago.

While Riddle was making up his mind as to whether or not he should take an interest in the hotel, he got a phone call from Bill Miller. Bill Miller, like Jack Entratter, was an old pro at booking entertainment.

Major Riddle recalled in 1979:

[Miller] encouraged me about the possibility of bringing top acts to the hotel. So through his insistence, we formed M & R Investment Company with Miller as president and myself as vice-president. However about a year later we began to disagree about the running of the hotel. So I bought him out.
Las Vegas Sun Sunday Magazine, July 15, 1979

The Dunes Hotel and Casino re-opened on June 6, 1956, and the two new owners invited all the high rollers, celebrities, and movers and shakers in town. Miller and Riddle had an idea for making the hotel more financially stable. They had entered into a contract with the famed Minsky's Burlesque to bring the *Minsky's Follies* to the Dunes. Minsky's was famous not only for their burlesque queens but for the stripping acts that the girls performed as well, and when the exciting new show re-opened the Arabian Room, it featured Lou Costello, of Abbott and Costello fame, as the star.

The uproar was immediate. Local Catholic priests, the Legion of Decency, and city and county officials were fielding angry phone calls from protesters while

The young women of *Minsky's Follies* at the Dunes. Image courtesy of UNLV's Special Collections.

the state legislature were all up in arms. Bare-breasted girls were on stage in Las Vegas—the newspaper editorial pages were filled with columns denouncing the move away from more wholesome entertainment.

With somber faces and hearts on the bottom line, the community was worried that it would bring the wrong element to Las Vegas while overlooking the obvious. Even an old booking pro like Jack Entratter weighed in with the opinion that Minsky's was not suitable for Las Vegas.

Miller and Riddle didn't care. In the first week, it set a record for attendance, 16,000 patrons lined up, handed over their cash, and alleviated all that fear, and that attendance record held until the 1990s. The show was a smash and ran for an unprecedented six weeks. Gamblers were more than happy to stay around and to gamble after seeing the show. *Minsky's Follies*, in various editions, played the Dunes for the next four-and-a-half years.

The gamble paid off big time. The hotel began to slowly stand erect on its financial solvency. An office for reservations was opened at 204 N. Beverly Drive in Beverly Hills, CA, as many of the Las Vegas hotels had reservation offices on Wilshire or Beverly Drive in tony Beverly Hills. That office remained operational until the late 1980s. Over the years, Riddle had the logo updated and made it more eye-catching and colorful.

A young Minsky's dancer makes a phone call. Image courtesy of UNLV's Special Collections.

Pinky Lee, a vaudeville comic and television host, was the star of the *Minsky's Follies* in the summer of 1958. He broke Lou Costello's six-week run record by being held over to standing room only crowds for eight weeks.

But finances were always on Major Riddle's mind. In an interview he gave in 1958, he was quoted:

> The physical problems are always pressing. Take that pool of ours, we pump 285,000 gallons of water a day into it, all of it from our artesian wells. And air conditioning, keeping an establishment of this size about 45 degrees cooler, 24 hours a day for about six months a year costs so much I don't want to think about it. Then there is the maintenance, the payroll, food, drink and entertainment—all of which must be run at a loss.
>
> *Fabulous Las Vegas Magazine*, March 1958

Riddle went on to lament that gambling costs at the Dunes for the nine-month season were exorbitant. It was becoming harder and harder to draw tourists because of all the choices they had for accommodations. The hotels were in a never-ending competition for those dollars. Riddle said that the Dunes needed more rooms. He hinted that a twenty-story tower would be added to the property which would be the tallest structure in Nevada. He envisioned it having a 1,500-seat convention center that would rival the then under-construction Convention Center being erected nearby on Paradise Road. The tower would also have nursery facilities, a 1,000-seat dining room, a gym, and at the top of the tower would be a lounge called the Top o' the Strip. Riddle believed that if you "could get the rooms, you could get the tourists" and once you had the tourists, you could make a profit.

In 1959, Riddle opened the famed Dunes Golf Course and Country Club. He had insisted upon having a golf course styled after the one at the Desert Inn. He also saw how that hotel's Tournament of Champions helped bring publicity and tourists to the hotel. He purchased additional land from Dunes Road to Tropicana Avenue from Mel Close and banker Jerry Mack. Called the Miracle Mile, the course was an 18-hole, par-72 layout among a sea of emerald green.

In April, Riddle presided over the groundbreaking for the new convention facility he had dreamed of. It would be 6,600 square feet and accommodate conventions, trade shows, and public meetings.

In May, Harold Minsky signed a two-year extension contract to continue to produce shows for the Dunes at $100,000 per annum. In July, the Aztec Birdmen, who performed ritual dances on a platform atop a 100-foot pole, replaced the Flying Indians of Peru, a diving group. To add to the excitement of the performances, safety nets were not installed.

The Dunes marquee in 1956. Image courtesy of the J. Florian Mitchell Collection, Nevada State Museum, Las Vegas.

As the 1950s were coming to close, Riddle had ambitious plans for the hotel but he still faced financial difficulties, which would require taking on partners.

However, Riddle was already busy making plans.

A FRENCH INVASION

As the 1960s unfolded, Major Riddle's plans for the Dunes Hotel included bringing a spectacular French revue to the showroom, but before making the investment, he decided to test the waters.

Vive Les Girls! was the show he would anchor in the Parisian Room Lounge. He hired Frederic Apcar to produce the show. Apcar and his wife, Florence, had been adagio dancers in the famed *Folies Bergere* in Paris, and together, they created one of the most lavish production shows for its day. *Vive Les Girls!* also became one of the longest running shows on the Strip. Cassandra Peterson of Elvira fame would one day dance in the show on her way to Hollywood.

The Dunes Hotel souvenir program for *Casino de Paris*. Image courtesy of As We Knew It: Classic Las Vegas Collection.

The costumes and scenery were lavish, as the feather budget alone was rumored to be in excess of $165,000. *Vive Les Girls!* was so successful that Riddle continued his plans to bring a French spectacular to the Dunes.

Another of Riddle's innovations that year was the opening of the Sultan's Table, the hotel's gourmet room. It opened on March 4, 1961, and Diner's Club hailed it as "America's finest and most beautiful new restaurant."

The Sultan's Table was inspired by the Villa Fontana in Mexico City. Riddle had dined there once and was taken with the restaurant's atmosphere. He had enjoyed listening to Arturo Romero's Magic Violins and imported them to play the Sultan's Table. The chef, Jean Bertraneau, was from Beverly Hills, and the *maitre d'* was Joaquin Norriega. The restaurant was a success from the day it opened. Its "snob appeal" quotient was through the roof and celebrities made a point of dining there when in town. The Sultan's Table, catering to the "see and be seen" clientele, offered, "Continental dining in a romantic atmosphere with cuisine to delight the world-travelled gourmet. All modestly priced!" But even celebrities who didn't care about "modestly priced" fare like Elizabeth Taylor and Richard Burton often had their dinners sent over from The Sultan's Table when they were in town.

Major Riddle's Diamond of the Dunes Tower signaled that the Dunes was keeping pace with the other hotels on the famed Strip. Image courtesy of the J. Florian Mitchell Collection, Nevada State Museum, Las Vegas.

Perhaps Riddle's biggest innovation was his prized Diamond of the Dunes high-rise tower. The tower would help bring a new clientele to the Dunes, but it was a few years off. In the meantime, Riddle publicized the opening of the Olympic Wing, which included a new Olympic-sized pool and an additional 250 rooms. The Dunes now had 450 garden-style rooms, but the front of the Dunes still had the famed Sultan atop the main entrance.

The Arabian Room boasted such stars as George Burns with Ann-Margaret as his opening act, Carol Channing, Frankie Laine, Tony Bennett, Patti Page, Polly Bergen, and Eleanor Powell.

The Parisian Room was anchored by the over-the-top *Vive Les Girls!* still drawing nightly crowds with its no cover, no minimum policy.

The Sea-Horse Wing of the hotel featured (according to the ads) "Luxurious cabana rooms with a sun-deck overlooking the Sea Horse pool and the Parisian gardens as well as delightful bedrooms and magnificent suites just steps away."

The Olympic Wing and Pool featured the new Olympic-sized pool, making the Dunes the first hotel on the Strip to offer two pools. The Olympic Wing also featured regular rooms and suites.

The Convention Facility claimed to be the "most modern and efficient Convention Hall in America" and adjoined the Dunes large Exhibit Hall. According to the promotional brochure, "the ultra-plush marble titled Executive Conference Room is ideal for important Convention board meetings and business sessions."

The Aladdin Room offered a nightly buffet that featured a "tantalizing array of delicacies of over 50 items including piping hot dishes, beverages and dessert," according to a hotel brochure.

Riddle's innovations were costing a lot of money though, and Riddle himself soon needed more cash. When he went looking for investors, he sold 50% of his stock to veteran gamblers Sid Wyman and Charles Rich, as well as Wendell Fletcher and George Duckworth. Duckworth had invested, at various times, in the Sands, the Riviera, and the Royal Nevada.

With new investors, Riddle held groundbreaking ceremonies on October 20, 1962, for his Diamond of the Dunes tower. Governor Grant Sawyer, Congressman Walter Baring and Clark County Commissioners were on hand. The tower would cost $8 million to build.

With the groundbreaking done, Riddle was still thinking about the French spectacular that would anchor the new showroom. Riddle approached Frederic Apcar about possibilities. Apcar suggested that the famed *Casino de Paris* be brought over. Riddle sent Apcar to Paris to persuade show producer Henri Varna. Varna was eighty-four years old and thought the only city that mattered was Paris.

According to Frederic Apcar, "Varna felt that to send his show out of the country would be like sending a national treasure to be debased." But Varna did admire Apcar and agreed to talk with him. (*Las Vegas Sun Sunday Magazine*, July 15, 1979)

Before coming to America, Apcar had befriended Line Renaud, who was now the star of *Casino de Paris*. Varna adored his star and Apcar now promised her that if she came to America as the star of the show in Las Vegas, he would make her an international superstar. Renaud and Apcar convinced Varna to at least visit Las Vegas.

Dunes publicist Lee Fisher recalled the visit in a 1979 interview:

> I remember when we picked Varna up at the airport and took him into the casino. We gave him a nickel to play a slot machine. He jackpotted. Then we gave him a dime. He jackpotted again. We gave him a quarter and he jackpotted

Postcards were sent out advertising the new *Casino de Paris* show at the Dunes. Image courtesy of UNLV's Special Collections.

a third time. Varna simply never had a more exciting time in his life. He was captivated by Las Vegas.

Las Vegas Sun Sunday Magazine, July 15, 1979

Riddle convinced Varna that the Dunes would do justice to the "heritage of the *Casino de Paris*." Varna countered by reminding Riddle that he did not need Varna's permission to use the concept or the name of the show. Riddle replied "if we can't bring a legitimate and authentic *Casino de Paris* to Las Vegas, then we'd rather not offer it to the American public. We prefer to pay for the cost of the original rather than pay for an imitation." (*Las Vegas Sun Sunday Magazine*, July 15, 1979)

Varna was sold, and Riddle had his French spectacular. The Apcars went to work on producing an authentic version of the show. An octaramic stage was designed and built in Scotland for the show. Riddle imagined the show in his new showroom once the Diamond of the Dunes tower was completed.

In the meantime, Riddle continued to get publicity for the hotel. Steve Allen featured the hotel on ninety-minute special he was doing for network television. United Artists held the world premiere of *Love is a Ball* at the Huntridge Theater near downtown. Allen filmed segments at both the Dunes and the theater.

Riddle appeared on *The Tonight Show with Johnny Carson* where he talked about his latest promotion, *The Weekend Gambler's Handbook*. Phone calls flooded into the hotel from around the country with people asking for copies. The first printing of the *Handbook* sold out.

In the spring of 1963, Floyd Patterson was preparing for his upcoming bout with Sonny Liston, and he used the Dunes as his training camp. The heavy-weight championship fight was held at the Las Vegas Convention Center's Rotunda.

On November 29, 1963, Riddle announced that Frederic Apcar and the cast of *Casino de Paris* were coming to Las Vegas. The show was scheduled to open on December 23, a relatively quiet time on the Las Vegas Strip. Christmastime found many hotels shutting their showrooms as tourism dropped off dramatically prior to the holiday and would not pick up until New Year's Eve grew closer.

The *Casino de Paris* was a success. Apcar stayed true to his promise to its star, Line Renaud. The show made her an international superstar.

In May 1964, the beloved Sheik was removed from the roof of the hotel and placed into storage. The hotel underwent structural changes as the new "Diamond" tower began to rise. The Sheik would be brought out of storage once the new interstate freeway, I-15, was completed. He would be placed on the back of the Golf Course near the freeway exit for Dunes Road and encourage motorists to exit now for the Dunes Hotel.

A new neon sign was added to the front of the property that year. Designed by Lee Klay of Federal Sign and Signal Company, the Dunes sign was 180-feet tall and shot neon into the heavens as flicker bulbs lit up the word: Dunes. The sign's foundation was 80 feet wide, and it took several miles of neon tubing to light. Three fulltime service men were hired to care for the sign.

The onion dome at the top of the sign evoked, according to author Alan Hess, "a Thousand and One Arabian Nights fantasy but when it is read as a stylized spade, the sign reflects the roadside tradition of buildings in the shapes of the things they sell." (Alan Hess, *Viva Las Vegas: After-Hours Architecture*)

The sign cost $250,000 to design and fabricate. It was, until the later 1970s Stardust sign came along, the tallest free-standing neon sign in the world.

The architect of the Diamond tower did not like the sign. Milton Schwartz, of Chicago, objected to the size, shape, and placement of the size in relationship to his tower. He had designed a spire sign that tied in with the new *porte cochere*. Major Riddle however, wanted a sign that could be seen for miles and was in keeping with the neon fantasy land that the Strip was becoming. Schwartz fought but Riddle prevailed. Because of the cost of the sign, Riddle leased the sign on a yearly basis. The contract was for thirty years at $5,000 a month. (*Las Vegas Sun Sunday Magazine*, July 15, 1979)

The worker gets closer to the top of the Dunes sign while it is under construction. Image courtesy of the J. Florian Mitchell Collection, Nevada State Museum, Las Vegas.

The Dunes sign lights up the Las Vegas sky at night. Image courtesy of As We Knew It: Classic Las Vegas Collection.

The Diamond of the Dunes would more than double the number of rooms available at the hotel. The addition was designed, like many of the older properties going vertical, for the tourist that arrived by jet as McCarran Airport had opened a new jet-age terminal in 1962.

The event that set the remodel of the Dunes apart from the entirety of the burgeoning Strip was its master plan for the resort, which called for an additional five towers to be built over the years with the intention of the Dunes becoming a major player in the resort market. Schwartz, a graduate of the University of Illinois, "designed the kind of well-crafted mainstream modern buildings in which Chicago specialized," according to Alan Hess.

Co-owner Jake Gottlieb, who lived in Chicago and admired the work that Schwartz had done on the Executive House there, enlisted him to craft the new sections. It was Schwartz who eventually had designed the Olympic Wing and the Sultan's Table.

The Diamond of the Dunes tower, though it was a concrete frame structure, was creased on two broad sides. Alan Hess described it, "like the side panel of 1963 Buick Riviera … and it appeared machined like the Executive House in Chicago." (Alan Hess, *Viva Las Vegas: After-Hours Architecture*)

Deeply inset balconies protected the windows from the glaring heat of the summer sun. The Top O' the Strip nightclub and a health club occupied the penthouse. There was an *Alice in Wonderland*-themed nursery as well. "Without possessing the Landmark's techno-romance or the Desert Inn's prosaic up-to-dateness, the Dunes managed to project the elegance and progressiveness of Modernism." (Alan Hess, *Viva Las Vegas: After-Hours Architecture*)

Schwartz redesigned the *porte-cochere* and added a second, high-end restaurant, the Dome of the Sea, a clamshell of a room "suspended from six legs of sculptured concrete by a web of stainless steel and threads. The legs sat in a free-form pool of water that reflected onto the bowl-shaped underside of the structure." (Alan Hess, *Viva Las Vegas: After-Hours Architecture*)

Sean Kenney, the designer of the restaurant, projected fish, seaweed, and subaqueous images on the wall. There was a small stage that held harpist Kippy Lou, who was dressed as a siren. Schwartz specified that she be 5'6", blonde, dressed in gold and white, and she was to sit in a large seashell that moved through a pool on a figure eight track.

The porte-cochere was anchored to the Dome of the Sea with its twin tapering pylons sweeping upward, giving a visual sense of dynamic lightness. Schwartz designed it while flying back and forth from Chicago. The five-hour trip left him plenty of time to think. He told author Alan Hess, "It was my feeling of what it would be like to enter this fabulous world." (Alan Hess, *Viva Las Vegas: After-Hours Architecture*)

The Dome of the Sea restaurant at the Dunes Hotel. Image courtesy of As We Knew It: Classic Las Vegas Collection.

The interior of the new tower featured modern materials like stainless steel for elevator doors and stainless-covered carbon steel rods suspending floating stair treads balanced by rougher, more colorful materials such as the ceramic tiles used to accent walls.

Jake Gottlieb flew to Las Vegas frequently to chart the progress of the tower. He approved everything. He worked with Major Riddle to upgrade the clientele of the hotel. Both men wanted to attract well-heeled gamblers and high-rollers. Major Riddle worked a contract with junket entrepreneur (and Las Vegas legend) Julius "Big Julie" Weintraub to bring New York gamblers to the Dunes.

Prior to the debut of the Diamond, the Emerald Green Golf Court had its opening ceremony in April 1965, and extended the golf course to the back property line, which could be seen from the new Interstate freeway, I-15.

On June 4, 1965, the nightclub atop the Diamond tower officially opened. The Top O' the Strip featured entertainment from noon till 4:00 a.m. The Queen Elizabeth buffet, featuring roast prime rib of beef at a cost of $3.75, was served at lunch. The Russ Morgan Orchestra anchored the entertainment. International pianist Mafalda and her trio performed there nightly as well as at the Sultan's Table.

The Dome of the Sea opened a week later on June 12 with film legend Cary Grant flying in for the opening of the new restaurant. He liked the Dunes Hotel and previously had stayed there when visiting the city. Grant married actress Dyan Cannon there, and Jane Fonda wed French filmmaker Roger Vadim at the Dunes, as well.

Rouvan onstage performing in *Casino de Paris*. Image courtesy of UNLV's Special Collections.

The *Casino de Paris* moved into the new showroom. The show had been a success from the moment it opened. As in Paris, Line Renaud was the star. For one particular number in the show, she entered from the back of the house because the train of her Jose Luis Vinas costume stretched from there to the stage.

In 1967, Apcar added Rouvan to the cast. Rouvan was a powerful opera singer and he, too, became an international star thanks to Apcar. He signed a three-year, $1.5 million contract. Rouvan was born James Haun, but chose the stage name instead. The highlight of his performance, according to George Stamos, "was his rendition of *Vesti la Guibba* from *Pagliacci*." He was said to be the heir to the musical throne of Caruso and Mario Lanza. (*Las Vegas Sun Sunday Magazine,* July 15, 1979)

Audiences adored him. He became the first artist to star in two successive editions of Apcar's extravaganza. Rouvan would likely have had a storied career but he died in 1975 at the age of forty-three after a prolonged illness.

In 1968, Riddle completed an exchange of stock with M & R Investment and Continental Connector Company located in Brooklyn. As a result, Continental Connector became the Dune's parent corporation. Not long after that, Meschulam Riklis and Isadore Becker, owners of the American International Travel Service and the Riviera—at the time—purchased 30% of Connector stock to gain control of the hotel. Riddle, however blocked them by teaming with Irving Kahn, a prominent Dunes stockholder.

After Kahn's death, Riddle's attorney, Morris Shenker, arranged with Kahn's estate to buy their client's interest in Continental Connector. Thus, Shenker became chairman of the board and chief controlling officer. Shenker and Riddle continued to work together as the 1960s came to close.

They had big plans for the Dunes as a new decade was dawning.

STORM CLOUDS AHEAD

As the 1970s dawned, the Dunes was still a jumping place to stay and to gamble. Rumors, however, were flying around that Howard Hughes was interested in buying the property. Hughes had come to town in 1966 for a brief visit. The brief visit had turned into a much longer stay and Hughes had bought the Desert Inn rather than move out of the penthouse. Since then, he had been buying various Strip properties, including the Sands and the Frontier. Hughes

The Dunes in the foreground with Caesars Palace and the Flamingo in the background. Image courtesy of Bo Boisvert.

had recently purchased the Castaways and tried to negotiate with the Nevada Gaming Board. The Board had informed Hughes that he was teetering on a monopoly and would not be approved. Hughes offered to remove gaming from the Castaways in exchange for buying the Dunes. The Gaming Board said no.

In August 1971, the curtain finally came down on *Vive Les Girls!*. The show had been running for almost ten years and was a bigger success than Riddle and Apcar had ever imagined. Riddle had big plans and announced a $2 million remodeling of the casino and other public areas of the hotel. The remodeling would begin with the Parisian Room Lounge. On August 30, at the end of the 2:30 a.m. performance, the curtain came down until the remodel was completed.

The casino was enlarged, adding an additional 2,000 square feet and included automatic doors for easier access. A cocktail lounge was added next door to the Dome of the Sea. The baccarat room was enlarged and partially enclosed. Sixteen chandeliers were added to the casino.

Local architects Walter Zick and Harris Sharp, who had designed the much-loved Mint Hotel on Fremont Street, were hired. When the remodel was completed, *Vive Les Girls!* re-opened in the remodeled Parisian Room Lounge.

However, storm clouds were on the horizon. In 1976, Morris Shenker sued the Teamsters Union for $140 million. He claimed that the Teamsters had backed out of a $40 million loan to expand the Dunes. The lawsuit was dismissed but the Justice Department's interest was piqued as they were investigating the Teamsters, yet again, for its ties with organized crime.

In October 1977, the Securities Exchange Commission filed a civil suit against Shenker, the Pipefitters Welfare Education Fund, and the Pipefitters Local Union

The back of the Dunes Hotel and Country Club. Image courtesy of UNLV's Special Collections

#562 Pension fund, as well as sixteen others. They charged that the defendants had used $23.5 million in labor pension funds to help keep the Dunes on an even financial keel. Shenker, the unions, and eleven of the other defendants consented to charges without admitting or denying guilt.

Expansion continued in December of 1979 as the Dunes broke ground on a seventeen-story companion to their Diamond tower. The new tower would add 400 more rooms to the property, bringing the total to 1,300. The tower also contained luxury multi-level suites and landscaping.

Some good news came when the Southern Nevada Golf Association ranked the golf course as the most difficult. The eighteen-hole course had a championship rating of 74.5, putting it ahead of the Desert Inn and other courses around the state. A course rating is the degree of difficulty and is the basis for computing handicaps. The golf course was the biggest in the state and contained five man-made lakes which framed the fairway.

Long before today's idea that hotels are mini-cites, the hotels on the Las Vegas Strip back in the day started the tradition. Back then, patrons had to drive or take a cab from property to property. There was almost no walking the Strip as tourists do today. The properties were large with expanses of desert between them populated by small motels, gas stations, liquor stores, and coffee shops. The Dunes had vast expanses of free parking, two Olympic-sized swimming pools, a laundry and dry-cleaning plant on the premises, restaurants, gift shops, and a retail shopping area, all on 163 acres.

Shaking the rumors of being involved with organized crime figures wasn't easy for The Dunes. Shenker's ties to the Teamster's Union had garnered the attention of the Justice Department, and the hotel only fueled the rumor mill when eight members of the Colombo crime family stayed there in 1980.

On November 21, 1980, the MGM Grand Hotel, across the street from the Dunes, caught fire. The fire began in the Stage Door Deli and roared out of the deli and across the casino. Hotel patrons awoke to choking smoke and the sounds of sirens. As they frantically tried to escape the burning hotel, the Dunes opened its convention facilities to emergency teams that arrived to help care for the injured and traumatized Grand Hotel guests.

In 1983, the Dunes added the Oasis, a second casino that featured a glass front with neon palm trees.

It wasn't enough to stave off the creditors. In 1984, Shenker filed for bankruptcy with $34 million in debts. Valley Bank and a Californian, John Anderson, stepped in and bought controlling interest in the hotel.

In 1985, the famed Sultan, who had gone from being the roof-top Ambassador to the golf-course ambassador, encouraging drivers to visit the Dunes at the next exit, caught fire and was destroyed. The cause turned out to be an electrical fire

The Dunes sign and Oasis neon palm tree prior to going dark. Image courtesy of As We Knew It: Classic Las Vegas Collection.

in his belly. Also about this time, M&R filed for bankruptcy. Try as he might, Major Riddle could not work another saving play for the Dunes.

In 1987, Japanese millionaire Masao Nangaku bought the Dunes for $155 million. He promised major improvements to the property, but they never developed. The Dunes continued its downward spiral, unable to keep up with the new hotels being built, such as the Mirage. New improvements and additions would not increase its appeal to the regular clientele. There were rumors of mismanagement flying all over town, while the Dunes continued to spiral even further down.

By 1992, Nangaku had enough. For five years he had tried to liquidate assets to help pay for the $200 million needed to upgrade the hotel to make it competitive in the market of Las Vegas of the 1990s. But he was not successful. Others said he had pocketed any money that the hotel had made instead of spending any of it on improvements. Whatever the real story was, Steve Wynn bought the property in November 1992 for $75 million.

The Dunes closed her doors forever on January 26, 1993, at midnight. Employees danced to a calypso band and enjoyed free prime rib at the Sultan's Table before watching the giant marquee go dark. Over 1,300 employees were out of work. Many had worked there for over ten years and some as long as twenty-five.

The internal publicity newsletter of the Dunes, the Sultan Sez, heralds the end of the hotel. Image courtesy of Carey Burke.

All gambling was halted at 5:15 a.m. on January 27. Chips were collected and the coins collected from the slot and video poker machines. Gaming agents taped the coin slots shut and hung "out of order" stickers on the screens. The coins were delivered to the counting room, and the chips and cash were delivered to the main cage. Arthur Anderson and Company arrived early Monday morning to perform the final audit.

On April 23, 1993, Ed Hassen of YESCO dismantled the flashing neon palms on the Oasis Casino, and they were sold at auction and shipped to the buyer in Taiwan.

Steve Wynn was planning a huge celebration for the demolition of the Diamond of the Dunes tower. Taking a page from Kirk Kerkorian's original MGM Grand Hotel, Wynn planned to build a resort that would redefine luxury on the Strip. He called his new resort Bellagio and had plans drawn up for an European/Tuscan/Mediterranean facade that would have no neon and would evoke a feeling of visiting Italy.

But first, he had to demolish the smaller buildings on Dunes property.

On September 16, 1993, a construction worker driving a front-loader started a fire when he ran over an electrical circuit in the old garden-style motel section near the north tower. With winds up to 30 mph, the fire quickly spread. The four-alarm fire swept through portions of the Dunes, filling the Strip with black smoke and causing a partial evacuation of the nearby Barbary Coast. Employees at the nearby Job Center, which had been set up to help former employees find new work, were also evacuated. Caesars turned on their outdoor sprinkling system to protect their landscaping from flying embers. The Barbary Coast and the Flamingo were advised to turn off their ventilation systems to keep smoke from entering the casino areas.

The fire was first reported at 3:26 p.m. and within a half-hour had grown to a four-alarm fire—thirty-three fire units, 125 firefighters, and dozens of support personnel were called to the scene. Steve Wynn's brother, Kenny, who was directing the demolition, reported that all fifteen workers were accounted for and safe. His greatest concern was that the fire would spread to the south tower where Wynn management had moved many boxes of records and paperwork.

The Diamond of the Dunes tower caught fire from flying embers. The fire began on the fifteenth floor, but the firefighters got lucky when the automatic sprinkler system was triggered.

A fire broke out in the hotel's casino on the ground floor. Luckily, it was quickly brought under control.

Fires on the Las Vegas Strip always evoke memories of the MGM Grand Hotel tragedy, and this one was no different. The fire was contained by 7:00 p.m., but firefighters remained on the scene overnight to battle any flare-ups. A flare-up occurred about 8:30 p.m. in the southwest corner of the south tower, but it was quickly brought under control.

Controlled Demolition, the company in charge of the demolition, warned Wynn that demolishing a building was dangerous, and there was the potential for injury. Wynn listened, took notes, and continued to plan a big party inviting international news crews. Mirage spokesman Alan Feldman and the Nevada Highway Patrol encouraged people to stay home and watch the implosion on television. Nearby properties were concerned about the dust, and Wynn promised to pay for any cleaning needed after the implosion.

A huge fireworks display was planned as well. It was estimated that it would take the building twenty-five seconds to fall.

Wynn planned to throw the switch on the blasting machine, which would send 500 volts of electricity to spark the pyrotechnics and demolition. There were to be seven loud explosions followed by a huge fireball created by aviation fuel that would roar up the tower's east face. The sides would fall away and the center section would pancake down.

At the same time as the demolition began, the famed Dunes sign was to be blown up as well. Too large to move, the sign was a victim of its own design. Left in pieces, the sign would never work again.

The streets around the Dunes were closed at 7:00 p.m. on the evening of the demolition. Bleachers were set up in the front parking lot of Bally's, and I-15 was closed ten minutes before the implosion.

Bally's marketing department had a field day:

Get ready for the biggest blow-out in Bally's history. We're celebrating the demolition of the Dunes with megatons of casino fun, an explosive line-up of superstar entertainment and one gigantic blast—a free demolition party. The event will take place in Ballys' front lot where hot dogs, beer and soft drinks will be available for sale.

No one noticed the irony in the fact that Bally's had been the original MGM Grand Hotel.

On October 27, 1993, the demolition of the Dunes began. VIP guests were seated in a special section in the Bally's parking lot and given plastic ponchos, earplugs, goggles, and breathing masks. Wynn warned those with weak hearts and breathing problems to stand further back. At 10:00, Wynn returned to the stage to order the Captain of the HMS *Britannia* at nearby Treasure Island to fire its port cannons at the Dunes. Cheers went up from the crowd as the fireworks began, and the sounds of the implosion could be heard.

In the aftermath of the implosion, westbound drivers on W. Flamingo Road sit in traffic as the famed Dunes sign lies among the rubble. Image courtesy of As We Knew It: Classic Las Vegas Collection.

An explosion went off at the base of the sign and several fireballs roared toward the sky. A series of explosions rocked the tower. For a moment, it was motionless. Then the sign began to fall, and the tower began to pancake. As the building hit the ground, dust and black smoke billowed around. The roof had caught fire and was quickly extinguished. No one was hurt and only one person was reportedly treated for smoke inhalation.

It had taken 365 pounds of dynamite to bring down the building. Eighty-four flash bombs and 281 mortar cannons fueled the fireworks display.

After the Dunes fell, demolition parties became all the rage as property owners tried to reap the benefits of publicity for tearing down their original buildings to try and keep up with the new properties that were larger, more luxurious, and promised more amenities than ever before.

Over the next few years, more original properties would host demolition parties and revelers would whoop and yell as those original hotels met ignoble deaths. The party trend finally ended in the wake of September 11, 2001, and the original hotels destroyed after that tragedy did so with a subdued atmosphere.

As the Dunes was being destroyed, a new age of growth and a new way of doing business was being heralded. The remaining properties up and down the fabled boulevard had just received a very loud wake up call.

The Dunes sign towers over the Las Vegas Strip. Image courtesy of the Nevada State Museum, Las Vegas.

EPILOGUE

The Las Vegas Strip of the 1940s and 1950s has always had a hold on our imagination. Up and down the Strip, the hotel marquees advertised top-drawer entertainment choices and you never knew who you might run into while gambling. Sammy Davis, Jr., used to like to get behind a gaming table and deal cards to the guests. Sinatra and his entourage, like Elvis Presley, used to enjoy going to the lounge shows. Foxy's Deli, across the street from the Sahara, was often filled with some of the biggest names in comedy, especially early in the morning. It was the original 24/7 town.

That's all gone now, but the stories and the mystique thankfully live on.

The men and women I interviewed for this book were all a part of that era. Some worked in the hotels, some went to the Strip for a night on the town, others designed the huge signs that shot neon into the nighttime skies. They all lived in Las Vegas, many having grown up there. They each had unique stories to tell.

I videotaped the interviews and used parts of some of those interviews as text in this book. The digital version of the book offered all the video clips as part of the book. That is not possible with a bound book. I have the video clips if you are interested in having them on a DVD. Just visit my website, classiclasvegas. com, for the details. They make a great companion to the book.

Image of the original human "eye in the sky," courtesy of the Nevada State Museum, Las Vegas.

BIBLIOGRAPHY

BOOKS

Alan Hess, *Viva Las Vegas: After-Hours Architecture*. Chronicle Books, 1993.

Ed Reid and Ovid Demaris, *The Green Felt Jungle*. Trident Press, 1963.

Geoff Schumacher, *Howard Hughes: Power, Paranoia & Palace Intrigue*. Stephens Press, 2008.

Katherine Best and Katherine Hillyer. *Las Vegas Playtown, USA*. David McKay Books, 1955.

Mike Weatherford, *Cult Vegas: The Weirdest, the Wildest, the Swingest Town on Earth*. Huntington Press, 2001.

Paul Ralli, *Viva Vegas*. House-Warven, 1953.

Pierre Cossette, *Another Day in Showbiz*. ECW Press, 2003.

Steve Fischer, *When the Mob Ran Vegas: Stories of Money, Mayham and Murder*. Berkline Press, 2005.

W. R. Wilkerson III, *The Man Who Invented Las Vegas*. Ciro's Books, 2006.

ONLINE RESOURCES

David G. Schwartz, *The Long Hot Summer of 1955*, Vegas Seven, Aug. 6, 2015.

Deanna DeMatteo, The LV Strip History website.

Jeff Burbank, Online Nevada.

K. J. Evans, A. D. Hopkins, and Mike Weatherford, *The First 100: The Men and Women Who Shaped Las Vegas*.

The Barbra Streisand Archives

MAGAZINES

Architect and Engineer

Fabulous Las Vegas Magazine

Harper Magazine

Las Vegas Life Magazine

NEWSPAPERS
Las Vegas Review-Journal
Las Vegas Sun Newspaper
Las Vegas Sun Sunday Magazine, March-December 1979.

ORAL HISTORIES
Maxine Lewis, 1987, UNLV Special Collections.
William Moore, *The Pioneer Tapes*, 1981, UNLV Special Collections.

Gentleman in the counting room with a handful of dice. Image courtesy of the Belknap Collection, Nevada State Museum, Las Vegas.